AF322720

Don't Eat Your Children

Quips and Tips from a Mom of Six

Mege Gardner

New Perch Publishing

For my beloved beans

Also by Mege Gardner

Undertakers, Harlots and Other Odd Bodies, a novel

Don't Eat Your Children

Contact the author: mom@askyermom.com

Gardner, Mege

Don't Eat Your Children / by Mege Gardner

ISBN 979-8-218-52651-1

1. Family and Relationships 2. Humor (nonfiction)

New Perch Publishing, Baltimore, Maryland

www.new-perch.com

Contents

Acknowledgements

Much of this book is informed by many years of reading, forgetting, relearning and re-forgetting a bunch of authors who touch on parenting, human development, psychology and helping yourself to other people's psychology. In no particular order, they are M. Scott Peck, Carrie Fisher, Frank Zappa, Charlotte Bronte, Viktor Frankl, Agatha Christie, Dr. Benjamin Spock, Madeline Miller, John Irving, Steven Covey, Thomas Hardy, David D. Burns, Emily Bronte, Gavin de Becker, Dr. Nicole LePera, Thomas Hardy, Dr. Susan David and everyone I forgot to mention here or will ever encounter in the future who reinforces the most helpful notions.

I would like to thank everyone who has ever listened to my complaints, read my complaints or been in the vicinity of tolerating them.

Sure, it seemed like a waste of your time, but your love and patience kept me just sane enough to get to the other side of motherhood, if not the other side of complaints.

Author's Note

Throughout this book, any names are probably fake and the pronouns are all she and her. This is primarily to protect the privacy of my spawn and step kids. Although embarrassing my kids is one of the greatest joys of parenting, I think it's best to spare them the awkwardness some of these stories might cause.

To further protect the privacy of my kids and other weirdos, all the examples will be strictly semi-factual. The kids may deny some of these stories because they never happened, or they honestly don't remember the incident. It's all fine. I am not a journalist, yet. Passages that seem like gossip are almost certainly fabrications, I'm sure.

It's painful to be honest about personal disasters, and not all personal disasters are ours to share. If we aren't embarrassed as we discuss it, it's probably not our story to tell.

No one actually impregnated a babysitter, or if they did, I didn't figure it out. Yet. It's one of those aforementioned embellishments to spice up the true parts with unnecessary drama.

If you think you are one of the men in this story, relax. If you are alive and reading this, you are not going to be critiqued in here. I have already spent enough time figuring out what is wrong with you, I don't need to tell everyone about it.

I want you to thrive and never fear I'm going to wring out your ego or hang it out like a flag. That's your job.

I use the word *kids* throughout, as my preferred euphemism for *human children*. If you are bothered by goats, this may not be the book for you, as it will get your goat, so to speak. I learned the hard way that some people have a deep dislike for being referred to as *kids*. If you are one of them, I cannot be more sorry, kids.

Worse still, my first obstetrician used all the corniest euphemisms, like *bun in the oven* and *ankle biter*. I don't like those, and I didn't like him. Shortly after indifferently presiding over my first birth, he lost his medical license.

It was probably because of the euphemisms.

Finally, if digressions give you hives, this may not be a book you want to pay money for. Perhaps steal it from an enemy.

Moms like me do not write books like this, ordinarily. We do not write because we are so tired, and most of all, we are tired of talking about parenting and problems and pablum. We want more than anything to be able to afford a new liver so that we can wreck ourselves on a beach without consequences. We are ready to talk about sex in restaurants, flirt with gay waiters and make everyone uncomfortable. We no longer suffer the stuffy people who refuse to take our comedy seriously. We have become passionately obsessed about birds who have never done a thing to deserve it. When you open our refrigerators, there are zero casseroles and a scary surplus of cheese. No, we will not cook your dinner on Tuesday.

We have done enough of many things and if you ask us about it, you may need a new liver of your own to get through the stories—and that's only considering the birth stories. We have the gruesome and the heartwarming in equal portions because that is just the way honest, over-mothers roll.

The ideas are largely my own, I'm pretty sure. I have a list of influences in the acknowledgements you won't read and I will credit the bits that I am convinced should be credited. Unfortunately, I am proven fallible on this, having accepted credit for a George Carlin joke[1] for twenty years before I realized my error.

As I rule, I recommend skepticism for anything you see in print. Try to rely most on material written by folks who will lose their job if they lie. Do your research, check it out, and test it out before you saddle up your belief horse. If you just accept advice and information without critical examination, you will feel smart while creating stupid problems for everyone. I have test driven that particular horse for you, as have many other people with a collection of funky dilemmas. You can be smarter than that.

The chapters are a bit dense, so you may want to pace yourself to avoid brain cramps. A chapter or two a day before swimming is probably exactly what I would prescribe. Don't trust me yet? You don't have to!! You'll see.

---

[1] It's not important to tell the joke, but since I mentioned it, I feel it is my duty. Here's my paraphrase: "Just keep in mind that half the people are dumber than average." The original is better, but longer, so maybe not entirely better: "Think of how stupid the average person is, and then realize that half of them are stupider than that." Thank you, George Carlin. I know you are nestled with the comedy angels.

Some people will pick up this book in order to feel superior and craft mean messages about terrible parenting practices. Let's be friends, instead. You can still judge me if that's what makes you happy, I won't stop you! I can't stop you!

I'm not interested in judging other people's parenting, except for entertainment, so if you find yourself feeling defensive about any of my proclamations, remember, it's not your fault I'm bossy or mistaken. Carry on with love, or not!

You can yell at me if you really want to about my mistakes outlined here. That's fine if that makes you feel better about your own mistakes, but you won't make me feel any worse about mine.

It's possible people with childhood trauma will find these topics difficult, and I want to say, as a person with a lot of childhood trauma I am sorry that my style is too offhand about terrible things. Sincerely. It's how I've always coped—along with bouts of therapy, substance abuse and so on.

The alert reader will notice a smattering of God stuff in here. It's okay. You don't have to subscribe to my flavor of Jesus to help yourself to the meat of the material. That sounds kind of blasphemous, actually. Cool. We understand each other, I bet. God stuff has been tremendously helpful to me, but I don't insist that anyone else agree with my viewpoint. If you choose not to investigate God stuff, you have my blessing.

Among other mistaken concepts, *mistake* implies regret. It would be terrible and tragic to regret a whole person, so let's not do it.

I use *mistake* in the sense of misunderstanding. I am firmly in the camp of believing this: no one who fully and completely understands what they are doing would choose parenting another human.

The dip in birth rates where there is high-speed information available supports this belief. People are getting the message that other people are hard work.

Having children is a Rubicon-style[2] mistake, a point of no return, and no one who has done it can imagine the alternative. Once they have had kids, very, very few would seriously consider making a different choice if they received a perfectly functioning time machine; and isn't that bananas? Humans are the weirdest creatures, after all, even compared to the weirdest creatures we can call to mind.

So, let's hang up our regrets and not use the word *mistake* in regard to people. I prefer the word *surprise.* Currently, I have two planned children and four surprises.

Surprise babies can happen to you and your partner of the moment—to be clear, by "partner of the moment," I refer to the one you are boning. If you and the procreative partner are not scrupulously attentive to contraception, and even if you are, you can set your watch for a surprise.

----

[2] Mentioning the Rubicon or crossing the Rubicon is a very old saying that once you understand it you can't un-know it. The Roman army famously waded into a little river by that name and broke the law with no *take-backsies*, even if they backed up.

Other surprise kids can arrive when neighbors or relatives disappear and surprise kids can crop up when you live with a widow for a few years too many. Whenever you suddenly realize you have acquired more kids, you can consider yourself surprised.

I did not birth all the people I call my kids and they are fine with that. We are complicated in the facts of our relationships and straightforward in the spirit of being a family.

You don't have to untangle the who's who of it all to enjoy these chapters. When it comes to my partners—my husband and the subsequent gentlemen—you will not be expected to remember whose father is whose. I do, mostly, and that's good enough.

The Introductory Mistake of Not Reading Introductions

We took our fresh baby to a grown-up's urologist appointment, out of necessity. The busy doctor breezed in and introduced herself. Before we could say a word, she pointed at my then husband and asked, "Vasectomy?" Even though that is not his name, my husband nodded with a squint. She gestured at our baby, "Third?" I was very impressed.

Without explicitly telling us, she let us know people who have kids generally have one too many kids. Although she was very clever and experienced, she did not fully understand her audience. While my husband was done reproducing and sufficiently convinced of that fact to let someone maim his balls, I was still a fierce procreator who loved making new people beyond all reason.

I did go on to have a fourth baby and neither my first husband nor the clever urologist was involved. She warned us that vasectomies are not foolproof, but she neglected to instruct me that vasectomies are also non-transferrable.

In my universe, the first kid is a miraculous warm-up, the second provides misplaced confidence and the third kid gets your sanity. After the third kid, moving on to at least the sixth, all bets are off. It's a decade of diapers and the most sweeping science project of your life. If you care about money, you can't afford to keep caring about money and you will just have to get over it.

With my excessive confidence and gusto for breeding, it should not surprise anyone that I would eventually find myself the mother of six kids. It is very surprising, however, that they are thriving and supportive of one another, while I am enjoying the best mental health of my life.

I will try to explain how all that happened. I wasn't expecting to end up with half a dozen kangaroos, or anything, I just never expected all my kids to be truly okay and kinder to me than I deserve.

The mistakes outlined here are entirely my own. Because I believe detailing mistakes is the most entertaining and effective way to present instructions, this explains the structure of this book. I also believe no effort is ever wasted, particularly if there's a joke in there somewhere, hence my decision to make the effort to buckle up and write it all down.

Anyhoo, there are essential principles to parenting, and your intelligence, income, and good looks will not make any difference if you forget the basics. Unfortunately, people are incredibly skilled at forgetting the basics, and inclined to complicate situations when the simple decision not to be an ass can save so much time and trouble.

If you can keep just a few things in mind, you will get through the madness and discover you have a family you do not want to avoid. If your family can laugh at half the mistakes, you have done very well indeed.

Setting the challenges of parenting and step-parenting aside to unfurl my background a bit more, I can tell you my life has been difficult in the usual ways and in some peculiar ways. The successful vasectomy, while upsetting for my husband, was only the icing on the cake of an extraordinarily bad year that was so bad it went on for two years.

During that time, I faced financial ruin, cancer, near divorce, abandonment by my clan, and the loss of my childhood home. Getting knocked-up by surprise in the middle of all that was the only new bright spot, although it was a pretty scary bright spot.

Whenever I had a few moments to myself, I would slide to the floor and cry until the labrador licked my tears away.

Weeping was a regular hobby because I was isolated and uncertain exactly how I could support myself and my children in the future. The weight of my responsibilities began to feel like an endless avalanche that was crushing my life with too much life on top.

At the park with my third baby, herein referred to only as Pinto Bean, we balanced on a seesaw with the older gals. I realized at that moment, my own biomass and the biomass of my little beans were equal for the last time. This was only one of a thousand heavy thoughts included in my avalanche.

The only thing I was sure of was my own resourcefulness and my commitment to devote all that resourcefulness to motherhood.

This was not ideal, but it was the best idea I had.

I worked at a slow parade of businesses over the years, indifferently gaining skills in managing money and time and sometimes managing people other than myself. I had no professional ambition, but rather worked to be able to house all my little beans and try to keep them in a good school district.

It's exhausting to be single-minded for thirty years and I cannot claim I kept the one idea front and center at all times. Which idea was that? Oh yeah, devotedly adequate motherhood.

We moved often. Only my youngest had the same school pals through primary school. My two step kids enjoyed similar stability, but my other three had several transient tests of their resilience. One of our moves was executed like an evacuation and I suspect they still recoil at the sight of an unexpected moving van. Cardboard boxes and dollies make me uneasy, but I think that's just common sense.

Over several moves, we lived in a declining neighborhood full of widows and then a regrettable neighborhood where I was asked for directions to the crack house. We lived, shunned, in a rural area, and we then lived in one of the fanciest suburbs of Baltimore—yes, it has fancy suburbs, which may or may not also have two crack houses.

Based on my childhood, I am in no position to tell anyone how to raise their kids. I was raised by a group of relatives who were worried about leaving me alone with an unstable mother. They were not quite worried enough to stop leaving me with her, but other than that, they did well enough to help me reach breeding age and keep the party going.

Their homespun wisdom is both obscure and questionable. When I asked the best mother I knew what regrets she had, she said, "I would have always filled my gas tank when it was half full." One could take that as some sort of metaphor for self-care, but it's literal advice: don't drive around worried about running on empty. My people were practical like that. For the most part, I learned what not to do from the various parents who were nearby as I grew up.

There are no degrees on my walls, even though I have read and studied and forgotten enough parenting research and opinion that there ought to be some kind of extra-credit token I could flash like a badge now and then.

Someone told me I was very intelligent as a child, and I clung to that like a fact life raft through many stupid situations. None of this makes me truly intelligent or gifted in any way. That said, I can stand on one foot and rhyme beyond average. This does not seem a useful pair of skills.

So, while I don't have any credentials or the usual good reasons to sway anyone to listen to me, I have a tendency toward emotional exhibitionism and an excess of experience and compassion for the parenting experience—all of it. I have handled super-glued toes, supermarket jail, broken bones, intervals of bullying, sexual identity conversations, car wrecks, mysterious rashes, wild bashfulness and terrifying popularity— mostly on a very low budget.

If I am not an expert, this is not an expert guide. Being an expert won't help you much at all when it comes to parenting anyway. The simple fact is, you can be an expert parent and still get the wrong kid for your particular brand of expertise, or vice versa. It's not their fault, or yours. So few of us are granted the truly easy way to parent, that it may as well not exist. Parenting is always difficult in unexpected ways.

I am also not qualified to offer marital advice, although I do throw a pretty good divorce, if I do say so myself. Over the course of my parenting career, I restarted my life four different times with three different partners. There are good reasons this is not a recommended method, unless you are an exhaustion junkie.

My kids have put in 25 years of college, some of that time served concurrently. So far, we have five graduates, one post-grad, and one near graduate. There's no way I could have done that all by myself; we needed as many extra parents as we could get. There are some wonderful men who aren't married to me right now.

My therapy folder holds no diagnosis beyond depressive tendencies. I'm a teeny bit sorry for your sake that I'm not more interesting in terms of mental health, but having humor as a defense mechanism provides a boatload of entertainment. I love to share and share some more.

While I wasn't getting educated or professionally proficient at anything else, I quit smoking, drinking and shopping as methods to avoid contending with my own emotions. Eventually, I learned to face myself and my past and thrive contentedly on my own. Sobriety is not only fun, but it's the best fun you can have, honestly!!

Occasionally, I still berate myself that all that work took 30 years. Even if I am sober, I'm still a bit of a jerk, particularly to myself. Being a jerk is possibly incurable but there is still room for joy, albeit jerk joy.

I'll tell you what I know, and I'll try to cover the important parts more than once, even though I dislike repeating myself after decades of saying the same things again and again. Brush your teeth. Where is your other shoe? Nobody *needs* another cookie. If it's not fun for everyone, it's not a good game.

Chants like these can bring on the Mom Trance.

As I was saying, good parenting is essentially equal parts bravery, love and grace. If you maintain a sense of humor, file that under grace.

Chapter 1
The Mistake of Careless Motivations

Especially in times of collective neurosis, the existence of . . . mature people is of crucial importance.
–Marie-Louise von Franz

I have never met anyone else who had to start a survival fire using cotton nursing pads, but I know my people are out there, somewhere. The kids and I were only in a bit more than medium danger when I allowed myself and four of my kids to be marooned on an island in a big lake without even a small boat. We also, I realized, had no cell phone, not even a small cell phone. If anything else went wrong, it was going to go very, very wrong.

It was getting dark and there was a chance, I thought, that an upstanding person who cared about stray fires would see our fire and investigate our location. On top of that, it was becoming very dark on our island and I needed to be able to see if the splashes I heard were people or rocks or alligators.

The kids had a great time, and they do not particularly remember that protracted island evening. The eldest, at ten years old, stayed busy finding lizards and insects. Trees were climbed, a fire was enjoyed, the baby was fed, and no one resorted to cannibalism.

During this event, which was without a doubt one of the top three bad mom experiences of my career, I did not yell or sprinkle my panic all over the kids. I was truly terrified but decided not to behave terribly. It would help no one for me to act on my fear, intense as it was. Instead, I chose to outwardly relax as much as possible and stuff that fear somewhere safe for later. It was the most loving thing I could manage for them, until the boat eventually purred toward us, long hours later.

Mind you, I do not expect admiration for this feat of self-discipline, because I was responsible for putting us in danger in the first place. I only mention it as a vivid capsule of my parenting career: poorly planned, scary and freighted with the hardest kind of love and bravery, while waiting for unreliable rescue.

I learned a few useful things about parenting beyond the one evening, and even if you choose not to do it the hard way, you might learn from my mistakes.

Some of the details are upsetting, some are hilarious, and some are both.

Motivations

While I have plenty of tips and techniques for parenting humans in difficult circumstances, I believe there are only two or three ideas you need to understand and practice to be a pretty good parent. I was not entirely consistent on this personally: three ideas can sometimes be one idea too many to keep in mind in hectic times.

If you only have room for one objective, be kind, to everyone involved.

Caring for other people in every direction is very hard work and being kind to yourself about the imperfection of your efforts is important: it will conserve your energy for emergencies. Even if you don't have genuine emergencies, you will have imaginary emergencies brought on by exhaustion. It's okay. You've been warned. You will be ready to be unready.

Put simply: all the best parenting comes out of a clear motivation to act from love and bravery. Whatever emotions or pressures fill you, your actions should spring from love and bravery, not any of the other junk in there. The fact that you honestly desire to be a good parent is great, but it's like having fuel for rocket without a steering wheel. Rockets don't have steering wheels, I know, but you understand the point. You are so smart!

You may not end up where you expected to end up, but your efforts matter, always. If you keep your efforts lined up with love and bravery as your compass, most other things take care of themselves, particularly the situations you didn't have in your control in the first place. It's like spilling dog treats on the floor—it's only a problem if you don't have a dog handy.

You cannot ask yourself if your actions are coming from love too often. You may not feel loving emotions at a lot of moments, in fact you may have every other emotion boiling in your heart, but you don't have to feel love to act from love. These are very different things and if you are already confused, you are not alone. Some people never figure it out.

When I'm out and about and I see a toddler throwing a fit, I speak to them and say things like, "It's really hard being two isn't it? I can understand why you're feeling cranky. Candy is way too interesting." The parents don't always appreciate this, but they usually do because loving action is hardest in the moment of their own reaction to a tantrum. It also will typically make a toddler freeze in terror to have a weird old lady speak to them in the check out lane. They may abruptly remember they love their parent more than candy. Win win of love for everyone.

Love

Being motivated by love seems pretty self-evident. You may think, what kind of monster would act out of anything else? "Act from love" is so obvious, such woo-woo baloney!

Whatever your objections, if you intend to make some people and care for them properly, this concept deserves your attention. Seriously. Brush it off at your peril. You really don't need extra peril where you're going.

Acting from love is not easy or particularly simple. It doesn't mean giving and giving all the time or smiling gently in response to atrocious behavior. You don't have to greet toddler fists with a chuckling state of bliss— that's for later when you're a grandparent.

Acting from love will not always feel like a delight. Usually it's hard work, and like all worthwhile skills it takes practice. Most of us aren't born love virtuosos; we need to spend some time with our love fiddle to understand what it can and cannot do.

Acting from love means taking the time to sift through your thoughts and feelings about a situation and finding the most loving course of action. The choice is rarely the easiest thing; in fact, most mistakes come from taking the easy way and ignoring the inklings that are whisper-yelling at you to do one more thing you really don't want to do. Then again, sometimes the best, most loving thing you can do is leave everyone to their own devices and have a sandwich.

If you have ever sat still and listened to a seven-year-old tell you the entire plot of a movie jumbled and backwards, you know what hard love feels like. They want to share their experience with you, and you make the heroic choice to let them tell you about it and listen well enough to let them know they matter to you, and the thing they care about matters because they care about it. Whew. In this scenario, you are the real superhero. This stuff is a huge effort.

Recognizing a loving choice is incredibly difficult if you haven't been loved properly yourself. Get on that! Love yourself double-time. Don't fake it. Figure it out. If you get stuck, consider finding professional help to save time.

Love is confusing, and if you don't have robust mental health, the confusion will multiply faster than you can multiply people. Don't lie down in the ditch your parents dug. Make a better ditch!

If you have the choice between giving your kids everything and giving them mental health by example— you don't have that choice, because it isn't a choice. Mental health always makes the best gift.

My definition of love is stolen and simplified from Dr. M. Scott Peck's, which intones very precisely:

"Love is the will to extend one's self for the purpose of nurturing one's own or another's spiritual growth." That's a lot of words—possibly too many words to strap to our rocket—so let's boil it down.

For me, love is deciding to work toward nurturing greater development. Your decision to eat a healthy meal is love for yourself. That ramp you improvised for your arthritic cat to get into its favorite window? Also love. Working more hours so that you can avoid going home to your family might be loving your job, or not: what are you developing exactly? Are you working late to save lives or are you working late on improving some sort of weapon system? Maybe go home and cuddle somebody instead. You know what to do.

You can love other people while you love yourself, in fact, you have to. Nobody has time to sit in the mountains alone and do nothing but love themselves completely, until they are finally ready to descend on their family with all their love spilling all over the place. It happens in books and movies, but so do zombies. Fantasy is so confusing.

I'd venture that even monks have to avoid too much solitary confinement while they contemplate love. It's like loving only one part of an organism. You can't reserve your love for the hog's tail only. How's that hog ever going to get fed if you are obsessed with its tail? If the hog starves, you would both be love losers. You have to take a step back and really contemplate the whole hog.

When you love yourself, you make yourself more available to love others. When you care for yourself and make sure you have rest and nourishment, you get stronger and plump up your little Grinch[3] heart to do its Grinchy little love best.

It's easy to become confused and think the love supply can function in reverse. It doesn't. You cannot love other people to your own detriment and expect it will all balance out when they love you in return. All that does is plant a big old resentment garden, and that garden stinks while it grows relentlessly.

When you love somebody, you are making a choice to do so.

Oh yeah? Yeah! Don't get confused by fantasy on this point, either. The subject is love, not crushes and infatuation.

Anybody who has had an infatuation will tell you it's not the same thing as real love, and primarily it's because infatuation is not a choice. When you fall in love, you are under the influence of powerful brain chemicals and pheromones or things that mimic pheromones. They are there to entice you to try to breed with this person, regardless of any real suitability they may have. What if they have an enormous head or are otherwise highly unsuitable for your baby-making future? Your hormones do not care about any of that.

Believe me. I have fallen in love with laundry soap and deodorants and men with very large heads. There is

---

[3] The Grinch is a mostly misunderstood cartoon goblin who was so afraid of love and joy that it ruined a pagan holiday for some gerbils before it figured out it had the option to not be a jerk. It was created by the artist known as Dr. Seuss, who allegedly understood both love and being a jerk.

no volunteering for that kind of madness. Imagine if you had to have babies with everyone who used musky soaps! My infatuation malfunction was nearly that bad. Honestly, the aroma of love is all I can conjure to try to explain most of my youth. (Patchouli scents call up secret shame, but I'm pretty sure that's true for everyone).

Infatuation can lead to real and lasting connection, but it is just as likely to lead to waking up in a barn, confused and missing both your shoes and your twenties.

Listen to your loved ones when you are in that dangerous kind of infatuation haze; they can tell when your princess is a frog. Listen!

In the case of real love, you decide with your tippy top brain, not your nose or your gonads. You choose to invest your love in your love object because it makes sense in your life, and it fits in with the love balance of your love account. Everybody grows when love is on purpose.

Love is not about appetite; love is about nutrition.

There is an element of infatuation-like feelings for our children and it's lucky for them that it exists. We need to love those little suckers in both irrational and rational ways.

It's best to mostly stick with the rational love part, however. If you focus on the irrational love feelings, you can get mired in all the mine-mine-mine aspects of having a miniature you and that's no good for living in the real world of ours where they are in fact, not you.

Where parenting is concerned, we sometimes react out of embarrassment or selfishness, or we cannot be bothered due to laziness or the roar of our own pain. It happens. We are all very fallible.

We can't shut off our humanity in order to be some kind of parental love machine, and it's fine to be imperfect, as long as we keep making the effort to choose the loving way. We're not raising robots, after all. Humans need to see how real love is done.

Some parents work very, very hard at some very misguided goals. We see them at gatherings, and we don't always know how to avoid them quickly enough. Usually, they have a huge drive to control their kids, the kids have no privacy and seem pretty twitchy.

While their goal may be to keep the kids in line or to protect them from outside influence, they are actually making the world smaller for their kids. If the kids never travel, they will never experience looking back on their home from the outside. If they never brush up against new ideas and different people, they will stay tiny hothouse flowers.

Of course, when kids are kept in hothouse confinement, they can be stunted for a time, but it's only temporary no matter what their other limitations. Like it or not, adolescence has a way of busting all the glass and sorting out the bodies.

When you consider what "work toward nurturing greater development" means for you in regard to your kids, don't forget the "greater" part and the "work" part. It's not easy. If it was, everyone would get it right.

Bravery

While acting from love is tricky, acting from bravery is a little bit simpler, but very scary. Please don't worry that I'm going to spend a lot of time defining things, after this it's all sausage, no recipe, or something.

Imagine painting a mural for your entire life and working through thousands of tricky details only to discover that you never used any red colors because they intimidated you. You just weren't comfortable deciding where and how to use the reds. For a minute you were going to include a shark attack in that corner, but no, too red.

Acting from bravery should scare you like facing tangible and horrible possibilities. It's like painting that shark attack and using the red because it frightens you and it might frighten you again and again.

Acting from bravery means not hovering over your children and anticipating each misstep to prevent them from experiencing pain.

They are going to suffer in their lives. Isn't it better to be nearby to help them accept the pain and get to the part where they are stronger for it? (The exception is basic safety like childproofing. Toddlers are hazardous little tornadoes. You will want to get ahead of their path). Just don't reflexively get between your child and a minor natural consequence. If they are too rough on a favorite toy, maybe let them break it and then do not replace it right away. Especially if it's a noisy toy. Maybe the fire engine with the piercing siren sounds falls down the stairs so that they see how much stairs can destroy things.

But let's get back to bravery. Revenge is for later.

Acting from bravery doesn't mean there's no fear, just that you have considered the fear and chose to confront the scary thing anyway.

Acting from bravery is the natural opposite of *reacting* from fear. We are built to freak out and react from fear, after all. It's baked into our nature and has kept us from being pounded by birds of prey and gobbled by creatures with huge teeth.

I have personally had panic tantrums in airports and subways and hospitals. Those freak-outs were called for, probably, but it is typically not appropriate to have such an episode in the shoe store or the principal's office—or so I've been told.

Ration your panic. When you act from fear, it had better be an emergency. Sure, pull your kid back up onto the sidewalk because you are afraid of imminent doom, like a speeding car, but don't keep them indoors all summer because you are afraid of ants or other exotic terrors. Just because something can happen doesn't mean it's likely. You don't want to be the parent who is always using a pound of prevention when an ounce[4] would do.

If you constantly tell kids to be careful because of your own fears for them, you are doing real harm. Believe me, I was one of those jumpy kids who had to

---

[4] Ounces and pounds are used in an arcane system of measurement deeply beloved by Americans because they are so much fun to say aloud and are the delight of pouncing poets.

store up all my gumption for minor terrors like talking to bored cashiers.

Every parent has daily opportunities to stare down some very scary situations and imaginary scenarios. Some of us are tremendously skilled at cooking them up out of very scant materials. We're the ones who worry about birthday party balloons being a choking hazard. We can ruin any kind of harmless fun with the threat of ball lightning or kidnapping clowns.

My mother had a singular talent in making innocuous objects perpetually threatening. Seeing me in a long scarf she might say, "Isadora Duncan was strangled to death wearing a scarf."[5] I still credit that story with my otherwise inexplicable fear of convertible cars—a bonus fear.

Despite all the chances that come our way, we can skip some opportunities to terrify the little spuds; telling them balloons taste terrible and being proven right should be sufficient. Not oppressing them with our worries is the bravest way to host any kind of birthday party.

I can't claim to have anywhere near a perfect record on this point. Loving bravely wasn't really prominent in the mix when I got sloppy and rationalized some massively terrible ideas. Turns out, it's not a winning strategy to move your home every three years because it is time to clean the oven.

––––––––––––––––––––––––––

[5] On September 14, 1927, dancer Isadora Duncan was strangled in Nice, France, when the enormous silk scarf she was wearing got tangled in the rear hubcaps of her open car. How it took almost a century for this incident to be used in a horror comedy, I'll never understand.

Still, the times I got parenting right were the times I had the most clearly focused and loving motivations of all. Even feeling miserable for them in the moment, I knew what I had to do. Nudging some kids out of their comfort zones and standing firmly behind others while they took their consequences on the metaphorical chin, and most of all, listening to weird worries at odd hours— these were the most important decisions in loving my kids.

It's entirely possible that a colossally poor decision can be balanced out by thousands of tiny constructive decisions. I hope so. There's no guarantee, but there are very good odds that you simply cannot ruin everything.

All the sand from the beach of parenting can't possibly end up in your pants.

Fumbles

You won't believe me, but later, after you've screwed up your parenting mission, please re-read this, aloud, in a smug voice. Also know that it's okay to screw it up, it's pretty much the only way to parent effectively. The kids will never get what they need if you are endlessly

dithering about the next move on the chessboard of life. You will fail at some of it, so here, I made you a coupon for the occasion:

Very, very few of us will be objectively horrible parents. An even tinier fraction will be objectively recognized as the worst parents. It's incredibly difficult for conscientious, careful people such as yourself to imagine that you might forget to care for your children. Even so, the worst happens once in a while; some parents forget they have children or lose the plot in other ways. Perhaps they forget they can't really foresee the future, or maybe they simply didn't remember not to murder anyone.

Hey, please understand that if you get to graduation without any murder or active hostility of any other type, you did not do the worst job, and that is something— maybe not something to be proud of, but it's something all right.

You will be guilty of oversights, unconscious slights, and you will let the kids get away with things because you are just too tired from a long hard day of humanity. It's fine. You are allowed.

Don't pretend to have it all under control, because you don't, and you need to make sure you still have friends when it gets genuinely weird. When you level with people about your struggles, they might have something to offer. They usually do!

If you complain too much, nobody is going to be listening by the time you have serious complaints that are really worth the effort to spit out. You need to meter the complaints, particularly if you have broadcasting abilities. What if your final act is to post on social media that you just want a pretzel that is hot all the way through, just once for crying out loud?

Venting could be replaced with inventing, you know. Then again, maybe just move on without being too hard on yourself or the pretzel guy.

When you realize that too-vigorous play was causing all the baby barf, just bask in the knowledge that the baby is fine, and you will know better next time.

When it turns out that your kid had a broken toe instead of colic, maybe only wince for a few years. Everyone survived and their feet function and look perfectly normal. Probably.

Be as compassionate with yourself as you would with your very best friend, because this is a hard job and you couldn't know it would be like this. You can't really read the future, remember?

Intuition

Intuition is a very valuable gift. Some of us think if we have no parenting experience, we are somehow lacking intuition for it, but that's not how intuition works. It's in there, like your guts, to provide those gut feelings.

Whenever you have a powerful sense of the right path, don't dismiss it just because you aren't sure how you know what you know. Give your guts their due attention and dismiss them only if you have a truly better idea.

I distrusted crib bumpers, but we were gifted one and tried to make it fit in the first baby crib. In 1990 cribs were being designed with more and greater safety than ever before, but there were still antiques in circulation that could give the danger baby some options. Our crib bumper was supposed to pad the edges on the crib on the inside. It just didn't fit our bargain crib and bulged in all the wrong sections and flapped in others. I ended up tossing it, saying, "A kid could strangle on that thing, anyway." The first time I read about such an accident, I'm very ashamed to admit my horror was tempered by a tiny burst of pride. *I knew those things were trouble.*

Tuning in to our intuition can save lives, as long as we don't drive everyone crazy with it. There is a balance to be found. If we jump every time we have a sense that something is wrong, we'll be too busy jumping to get anything done. Perpetual panic is exhausting.

Your intuition will alert you when things are off. Just like you know a lot less than you want to, you know a lot more than you realize when it comes to parenting humans.

Perfectionism

Perfectionism is a swamp and that swamp is a trap. Even if you don't push yourself to be perfect, you also need to make sure you aren't pushing your child or partner to be perfect while you are giving yourself a break from the pressure of being flawless.

If you find yourself chiding the rest of your family about their half-baked efforts to help you, you'll be doing all the chores alone before you know it. The people you love want to know that you see what they are trying to do, even if they aren't always getting it exactly right, and by "exactly right" I mean your version of exactly right.

So what if Mom is continually putting mismatched mittens on the baby? The baby is the one who lost the others, anyway. Blame the baby, silently, and be glad she's getting out of the house at all. So what if Dad put the diaper on backwards? He did a thing with a diaper and if he's that inexperienced, he probably felt a boatload of anxiety about the entire effort. Be complimentary or just stay quiet.

The pressures of perfectionism have a way of shifting right along with your expectations. You push yourself along, up your chosen perfect mountain, and you tell yourself that any progress you make is no excuse to let up on the pushing. Maybe you someday reach the spot where you think perfection is perched. You stop only long enough to find some flaws. Maybe you tell yourself it's the wrong dang mountain after all!

Perfectionism is a habit of thought which will follow you everywhere, even all the way to the tippy top of Perfect Town.

Oh, I know, some perfectionists are thinking that it is the trait that drove them to succeed at whatever. Don't you want your brain surgeon to be a perfectionist? No, I don't. I want my brain surgeon to be well-rested and reasonably sane. The second-best brain surgeon is still pretty good.

For our purposes the point is: you are not going to be perfect and neither are your kids. Ever.

Parenting can be like getting a new, shiny, flawless thingamajig and being riddled with anxiety about scratching it, until you do. Now, I'm not suggesting you go around scratching babies, not ever, but try to skip the part where you dream you are going to lead them on a flawless expedition to ideal adulthood. Maybe pay attention to their little foibles and enjoy their imperfections. Those are the fun parts, anyway.

For the perfectionist, it is nearly irresistible to view their kids as having a shot at perfection. It is a purely exhausting and fruitless effort. Why not spend all that time and energy on something achievable, like becoming more interesting?

Performance

If you are too caught up in documenting your baby's every milestone and stunning accomplishment, you are risking missing out on all the other parts of your life, not to mention giving baby a very twisted concept of their own importance in the world. Nobody likes a self-important baby, particularly the grown-up, pompous ones.

The parents who spend all their time bragging and making a show of adoring their kids are the ones who aren't listening to the other people around them, possibly aren't noticing that their spouse is leaving them, or that their kid really believes they are better than everyone else.

When we have an ardent focus, our kids take note, and if we aren't aware of it, we can be slathering on the unintentional lessons. These lessons can lead to some really hideous unintended consequences, or sometimes sports.

When you habitually compare the achievements of kids, your kids will get the idea that you have some extra special, secret love for star hockey players, for instance. Your kids are always paying attention to what grabs your attention. Naturally, in this situation, some kids want to be the star and will be crushed by their participation medals. Other kids may become strongly anti-hockey in reaction to your achievement focus.

When we put too much emphasis on achievements and performance we can interfere with the most important growth. Kids need time to simply be, to exist, to be stupid. How else can they figure out who they want to become? We can't tell them, and even though we're pretty sure they have a hockey star destiny, it's not going to be possible if they don't see it and want it for themselves.

I pressured Garbanzo to try out for a high school play and I see and can admit now that my unacknowledged motive was to get backstage one more time. My own musical theater experience was mercifully short for the audience, but too short for my ego. Some part of me wanted to have a stage kid. I nagged. She grudgingly agreed. She did the show with magnificent energy and then quit theater for her real passion—the robotics club. While I still believe in her star quality, she chooses to apply it her own way, like a genuine star!

Wanting your kids to do well or at least improve a little bit here and there is perfectly natural, just pay attention to your attention and your pressure. You don't have to push them with all your own over-achieving juju. It belongs to you! You can't get rid of it that way!

Be present, be pleasant, and let your kid know they are just a peasant.

Chapter 2
The Mistake of Having Kids

We live in a perpetually burning building, and what we must save from it, all the time, is love.
—Tennessee Willliams

All ancient people had a moment when they finally became convinced that babies were not merely showing up by chance, like thunderstorms. In the usual course of events, people weren't being formed from spare body parts or mud pies or wishes on the wind. I would be willing to bet that whenever the most ancient human drawings are finally discovered, they will have nothing to do with aliens and everything to do with birth control.

Even people who are not fans of birth control will pine for it after a couple of kids. That doesn't mean they hate joy or want to interfere with human destiny; they probably just want to get some sleep.

Babies are great! Babies are also not great! They are designed to be utterly adorable and at the same time they behave in ways you would not tolerate from a pet or any other roommate. Imagine living with a grown man who screamed for you to hold him at 2 a.m. and then crapped in the bathtub every day. Maybe don't imagine that. It's unnecessary.

My grandfather, (the mailman, not the weatherman), was well known for a few sayings, the foremost of which was "Don't have any damned stupid kids." It took me a long, long time to parse this. I was pretty confident it was one of his jokes, since he said it in front of his own kids all the time.

Even believing he had been pulling my leg for my entire life, I felt exquisitely uncomfortable when the time came to tell him I was knocked up. It was a waste of time to worry, however. He seemed genuinely happy for me, and bestowed his cheeriest chuckle, which was still just a little bit sinister.

It is possible that he was laughing because he thought he knew exactly what I was in for.

Maybe he actually meant to say, if I should have any kids, they shouldn't be damned or stupid.

Kids are always stupid, even the smart ones. They are born knowing almost nothing, and it takes them a lifetime to pull themselves out of the stupid zone, if they are able. Some simply cannot be bothered to work on it and just loll around in their own brand of ignorance. It's possible to envy that dedication to the easy way, as long as it's working for them.

As for the damned part, I guess that's more of a spiritual or logical question. We are all born to die, but that's not the same thing as damnation. If they were the same, the phrase "death and damnation" would be absurd; it would just be like saying "death and more death."

Damnation is a distinctly Christian concept as far as I know. In order to avoid having damned kids, I could simply choose not to have any Christians.

If we were to go the Jesus route, we would have to get them baptized and hope they could live correctly enough to tiptoe away from Hell. Why not have some kids, educate them on how to be good, do right, and skip the Hell worry just in case Hell-worry is actually Hell? (These were just a few of the million or so musings I had about Hell and parenting; you don't have to agree with any of it. It's not on the quiz).

There's a famous saying, usually misattributed to Winston Churchill, "If you're going through Hell, keep going." This is very applicable to some phases of parenthood and also excellent advice for barging through life in general. It's certainly a better slogan than, "Don't have any damned stupid kids."

For my part, I prefer a kinder, gentler saying for my kids. I have always told them, "Don't get anyone pregnant," loudly, whenever dropping them at an event. Basketball game? Sure, whatever. Don't get anyone pregnant at the bowling alley, either.

They are mostly girls, so this was a source of amusement for most of their friends. I was serious, though, and I like to believe it's the reason I was not a grandmother ahead of schedule.

"Do you know what to call people who have sex?"

"No, what?"

"Parents!"

Having kids is hard enough when you have thought it over very carefully and come to the mistaken conclusion that you are ready. Being surprised by parenthood is never the best way to start out. Besides, there are much less expensive ways to terrify yourself and others.

Investigating

Now, I'm a narcissistic-leaning type, who was raised solo, so I approached family life the way a bird might approach fishing for the first time. I perched on a high branch and watched the other birds who fished for things. Oysters might be disgusting or delicious, after all. *Let's find out!*

My first ex-husband was from a big family, but he didn't like to talk about it. *What was it like?* I asked. *Noisy*, he said. And that was all he had to say about family life.

My mailman grandfather was one of six and would only say that the pranks were epic and the food was terrible. My other grandparents had siblings who had died, and I found my quizzes upset them. (I regret now that I didn't pester the other relatives. There are so many weird and wonderful facts for those who study families, and deaths are always very interesting).

My parents were both tangled in natal family bullying and favoritism, and they were bitter and confused about it, whatever it was. I certainly wasn't going to poke around and ask their sisters and brothers about any of that old mess. Again, this is a failing of nerve on my part. Oh, the dirt I could learn!

Even in my sparse research, I had heard quite enough stories about angry fist fights and being left behind at camp to believe I had the skinny on siblings. (As it happened, I did not, in fact, have the skinny on siblings, not at all).

Defenses

Before I started having kids, I polled every parent I trusted, so about four people: did any of them regret breeding?

They didn't exactly complain about their kids, but the pressure of their parenting lives was very obvious at times. They would usually have some update about the latest scrape of their latest kid, and they started many of their conclusions with, "I only wish…" as in "I only wish she would kick him out of the house."

Unanimously, these pressured parents answered me; having kids was the best thing they had ever done. Diva kids, sickly kids, whatever sort they had, they believed these were the kids they were destined to have in their lives. One of the moms said that she preferred motherhood had not given her a permanently weak bladder, but it was the only quibble she was willing to share.

People in America today are more frank about parenting than they were thirty years ago. Back then, there was this weird, soft, nostalgic bubble around parenting. Mothers were saints, fathers were splendid beings. If you scraped the surface of any television mom, she was basically the same person; super competent and ultra-patient and endlessly elegant. Please.

The covert scheme had been in place for countless generations: we must dupe the youngsters into breeding. Grandparents must lust for babies and tell stories that infuse their adult children with the gumption to get about making more people.

Sex was invented long before this, but grandparents really promote the stuff. I know. That's upsetting and I'm sorry. It's wasn't my idea. Old people have had more sex than all of the young ones. Just ask them, or maybe don't ask and worry about your own problems.

Even without pressure from your elders, you may feel the maniacal urge to breed and create life in the laboratory that other people call your pants. Think about it. Really think about it. Then think again.

How's your record with plants? Pets? Are you taking excellent care of your own body and mind? Your heart and soul? Are you ready to upend everything?

Maybe you have fantasized about selling all your stuff and backpacking or sailing to far off places. If so, consider that parenthood is the exact opposite of that. You will be in one place surrounded by a bunch of junk for a very long time. Sure, you can move, but it will be harder and harder as the roots of your life close in and as the cribs and play equipment begin to encircle you.

Coziness is part of living like a shut in; it's not all bad, not at all. It's just a teeny bit like jail, but cozy.

Consequences

Your little science project is going to be on you like a remora for a decade. You will not pee alone for nearly that long. Those lazy afternoons when you settle into mild boredom in the shade and flirt with the idea of a nap: they may never come again. Your sex life will be on the back burner in new and alarming ways.

While you decide whether or not to have kids, there are a couple of key points to consider. Having kids is basically handing your heart over to another person and watching them run around with it, as any number of parental people have tried to tell you. The little heart holder will potentially mistreat it. In fact, you are guaranteed to have heartbreak. It's a sure thing. For that reason, it's a very foolish thing to do but also an incredibly brave thing to do.

I don't believe there is a wrong answer to the question of having kids. If you aren't willing to donate your heart to another person who is guaranteed to break it, then you'll live a different kind of life and that's not bad, not at all.

You will find that there are plenty of other things you can do with your heart when you have the whole thing.

Skipping

You may opt out of parenting for any number of other reasons. It's okay, really. It's not the only chance you will ever have to hear someone fart themselves awake.

Maybe, like me, you will abruptly decide you want to have a baby, and then you won't get knocked up. Maybe, unlike me, you will take that as a sign that you should hang onto your vacation budget and your rabid reading habit instead of breeding. You're so smart! Your choices are also valid!

Your genetics might be a worry. There is plenty of great science for many scary inheritable diseases. If you have medical people who will tickle your DNA and knit you an enhanced person from it, that might be just the ticket to put an end to a long family curse. Only you and your money pile can decide.

There was nothing to be done, genetically, for my brood. They are stuck with long lives, during which they will be kept company by angry uteruses and depressive tendencies. At least they are tremendously good looking—the kids not the uteruses.[6]

In contemplating your possible parenting future, you might consider your general outlook. Maybe you have a dark view of the universe and would rather not have to read "Goodnight Moon" or "Frog and Toad" one million times. Those are both excellent reasons not to spawn. It's fine to go on and be dismal for a decade, without babies sprinkling in their contrasting cuteness and messing up your dark modern decorating esthetic with their unicorn toys.

Now, you may feel a tremendous pressure to generate progeny. That's natural too. Remember, however, not all natural urges are good for you. Don't pacify yourself with ideas like, "Bigger dummies have done it." That's true, but it's not the best justification for breeding.

---

[6] This is a clear example of the bias of parents. Possibly not everyone would agree that my kids are better looking than the average uterus. If so, they are well aware of the foolishness of trying to ever tell a parent such an opinion.

You really should have a much more colossal and sophisticated rationalization built up for your parenting choice. Maybe you'll imagine you are fully qualified and prepared and perfectly capable of growing good people. You're wrong, but it's so adorable and worthy that you believe it.

"No time like the present!" is not a colossal and sophisticated rationalization, but it's very popular just the same.

Compelled

Whether or not you opt to go on to raise kids in your home, you will probably be called upon to parent humans from time to time. You don't want to be the babysitter that is shunned by two counties, do you? Have some ideas to entertain them that don't involve explosives, electronics or negativity.

Some people look at kids and can only ask them what grade they are in. Don't be that neighbor. Ask them about their favorite books, their favorite bugs or what they like to do when it's hot outside. Ask them if they would rather be a dog or a cat or a bird, you know, the kind of things kids argue about.

Talk to them like they are real people, because, after all, they are. If you're up to it, be part of the adult squad they can rely on without undue bossiness.

It might be hard for you to be an encouraging presence if no one treated you like a human when you were young. If that's your origin story, you can feel extremely proud and confident as you turn down any babysitting requests until you have a nurturing comfort level. Congratulate yourself as you adopt a cactus instead.

If you do have to wrangle kids, understand that they will not always cooperate or try to please you. Have a backup plan for this, such as calling their mom. If you grab a kid by the ear, they will never forgive you, and rightly so. As a general rule, don't grab kids by anything unless it's the only way to prevent something much worse, like a sea lion attack.

Whatever you do, don't be fake with kids. Nobody needs that bullshit.

Teaching them how to silently low-crawl and pick pockets should not be your first choice to keep them busy. Also, do not get them to parrot psychologist's phrases, such as, "What does that mean to you?" until they are at least nine years old.

If you are going to hang around kids in any capacity, know what you are trying to do, and make sure your intentions are the best. Kids deserve the best.

Riches

You may feel some encouragement from seeing rich people who collect kids with ease, as if it's just a matter of money. Don't be fooled. Money doesn't touch the hard stuff, much.

The third kid will cost whatever is left of your sanity. Look around. Do you know anyone with more than two children who is arguably sane? It'll take you a minute to think of that *one guy*. Are you certain? Ask him about that third kid and what delusions he has, just to be sure.

There's another school of thought, of course. You may be the sort of person that really loves a good horror movie. Perhaps you relish those times you wake up from a sweaty nightmare and find that you can't move because, oh no, it's still a nightmare, only now you're frozen in place, pinned by the worst dread you have ever felt. Oh, wait. You're just a parent!

Instead of fearing creepy dolls that move around when you're not looking, you'll be worried about paying bills and keeping your own little creepy doll out of danger. She'll grin at you as she backs toward the edge of a dock and you will instantly dive in after her, even if it's the most rancid pool of water ever pooled.

Sure, with money you could afford to pay someone else to fish your kid out of disgusting situations, but money is easily the least important factor. Most people everywhere launch into parenting with insufficient funds, and then they are still broke for the next re-launch. They worry because they don't know all the things that money cannot do. Money isn't going to reassure you that you made the right choice, and money isn't going to drive you to the vasectomy appointment with a proper bag of ice.

Responsibility

The main consideration in deciding to have kids, which I did not understand until far down the road, is the real nature of responsibility. We don't have anything in our life without having the responsibility to care for it. Responsibility is the icing on the cake of your home and your hoard. When you are handed a live fish in a bag, the responsibility for it surrounds the transaction. When you discover it will eat all your other fish and will live for fifty years, the pet shop is no more than sympathetic, maybe. It's your fish now and you know you should have done your homework.

So it goes for all your major commitments to people and things. If you are going to fill your home with kids and dogs and then hire other people to be responsible for them you are still responsible for the outcome in addition to wondering why you set it all in motion, anyway. Even the fish will judge you.

Benefits

But hey, whatever. Purposeful sex is fabulous. Enjoy!

When your kids appear, you will love those little cabbages in a way that you never thought possible. Whatever feelings you have for your partner will be infinitely more complicated by the fact that your partner will become *just kind of okay* by comparison.

It can be infinitely depressing for new parents to realize the truth, so try to grasp it in advance: this is an all day, every day commitment for the rest of your life. You can't divorce your kids any more than you can divorce your lungs. If they are bank robbers you will be their first bank. If they are visionary wanderers, you will lose them in the grocery store, find them again, and worry about them forever.

Parenting gives you amazing and delightful opportunities. For instance, when a young person you have raised comes to you and says you owe them money, you can literally laugh them out the room. Truly. You can simply laugh until they leave to shake down someone else.

One magical day, you may hear your kids repeat your own advice back to you, which is even more gratifying than the mistaken debt collection. Borlotti Bean recently told me all about how to shop for insurance. I could only smile.

The joys—both the petty and the huge—make up for the grind, eventually.

Parenting will expand you, like it or not. You will do your very best for them and you will be certain that it's not good enough, at all times. Fortunately, it usually is good enough, even when you're a monster like me.

Chapter 3
The Mistakes With Siblings and Day Care

*When Dad found out they tied me to the goat, he was
furious. They thought it was worth a
beating and probably still do.*
– Some guy

For the purposes of understanding sibling relationships, I was essentially a spectator. There were large families around, even some huge families, when I was growing up, but their functioning was largely a mystery to me. How did anyone muster the courage to go down into the cellar to fish in a fluffy pile of laundry for clean socks? How could they wait so long for a toilet? Why were they so competitive about food? Somebody could lose an eye if there was cake on the table, and the carnage would not interrupt dessert.

Mysteries

Siblings seemed to be incredibly cruel to one another. At first, I believed that it was the individual big sisters themselves who were punishing their little sisters, but little sisters could dish out some brutality too. Boys who had bigger siblings seemed to lean either further into cruelty or far away from it.

Then there was the opposite dynamic, wherein the siblings would defend one another from outsiders, which could come as quite a shocking twist when one was the outsider. More than once I got a punch in the face for saying exactly the same thing a sibling had said about another; although to be fair, I used to many spicy adjectives and almost certainly had a punch coming.

Later on, I learned a few things from growing a set of siblings in my own home. For one thing, rivalry isn't automatic—none of the machinations of siblings are a given, really.

In fiction and in fictional family histories, people describe their relationships as one static thing. "My sister bullied me," or "My brother always looked out for himself." To my horror, I saw that brethren relations were infinitely more complex than a simple portrayal at any one time, and on top of that, they shifted over time.

Every time you add a person to the household, the population of the house doesn't just go up by one. When you add a baby to a two-person situation the headcount becomes three, but there are also suddenly three relationships also.

The second kid is, of course, just one more head, but that kid doubles the number of relationships in the house to *six*. Kid number three means *ten* relationships. By the time you get to six kids, you are dealing with *twenty-eight* relationships.

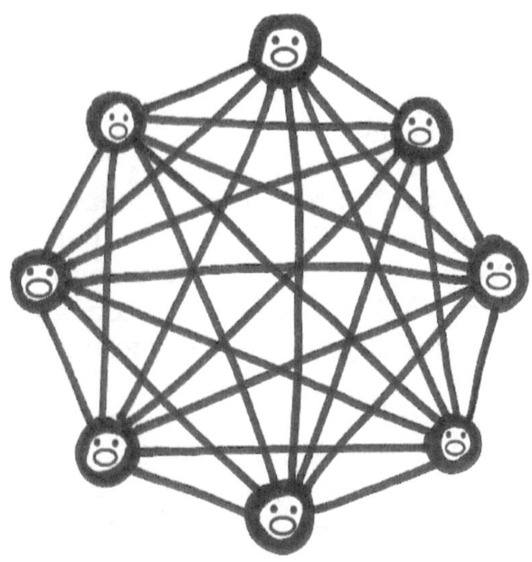

Christmas becomes a bonanza! Anyone getting the silent treatment will not care because they have a huge number of people with whom they are still on speaking terms.

Kid One may have good grasp on the norms you want to instill, but you may actually forget to teach Kid Four that they should look both ways before they push their brother off the sidewalk and that they totally should not push their brother unless he's about to be clobbered by a falling tree or a flying badger.

Now other moms will tell you that birth proximity does not guarantee friendships among the nearby kids. I agree with those moms. Closeness in age can inspire some fierce hatred instead.

When that happens, it's tempting to barge into the middle and try to resolve the conflict. If somebody ate somebody else's crayons, hang back and see if they can figure out how to work it out. Like any dispute, inducing vomiting is one way to go. You might discourage that, but most importantly, they need to learn how to negotiate and apologize as much as possible without grownups dictating terms.

You will want to set limits, remind them they are not allowed to employ violence, threats or treachery, and then step back. You will eventually find a rhythm for this that's effective. It takes a long, long time and it is one of the most exhausting mambos of motherhood.

They are going to attempt to pull you in to judge, particularly when the other kid isn't able to testify. One kid may have had the excavator all day long, but that testimony may well be skewed by another kid's impatience to have a turn. If you start using a toy timer, someone is destined to steal it and throw it down the well. Yes, you have a well in this scenario.

Even the most bitter battles can be nothing more than a phase. Keeping that temporary nature in mind is incredibly reassuring when the rage is fresh and loud. Nobody can keep roaring forever.

When the hoarseness takes over, do what you can to encourage them to move on to forgiveness. Encouraging is not forcing, of course.

No one should stall their relationship in a bad patch if it can be avoided. Of the more than twenty-eight relationships in our home, none of the kids' relationships have stayed mired in recriminations for more than a year. Yet. Those of us who aren't good at forgiving are really good at forgetting.

Do not force reconciliations with kiss-and-make-up dictates. That only causes kids to fake kiss and hate harder. You could insist they share a space without touching, or complete a chore together without speaking above a whisper.

I have bandaged children together to persuade them to be grateful they are not conjoined twins. Twin Time is a terrific distraction and an excellent threat for future quarrels. If you believe this is an abuse or waste of bandages, by all means do not try it. It works, though. Simply asking, "Do we need Twin Time?" has ended many scuffles before anyone could get scuffed.

There are, at least for my brood, particular ages which are the most annoying. For adults, coping with four-, seven- and eleven-year-olds can be delightful. My kids, however, were far from delighted with these particular ages of kids.

Most kids are at the cusp of big leaps of capability at those ages and they are naturally quite full of themselves. Total mastery of all things potty, reading and beginning to understand innuendo are, hopefully, happening in that order.

Because they are so full of themselves, this makes some intervals in a large family the stormiest. If you have a bunch of kids of these ages at the same time, essentially just figure that those twenty-eight relationships grew two heads. This happened several times for us. Even during the lulls, the kids closest to those ages were at the center of most any tempest.

While it is aggravating to live with, it was also a time when the kids could form intense attachments to each other. Our blended family really blended when a seven- and eight-year-old decided—voluntarily—they were twins for a summer. A shiny new big sister can be a fabulous bodyguard when you need one the most. An adoring little sister can likewise reinforce your hero status.

Maybe the whole point in your siblinghood is figuring out how to goad another person with a well-placed eyebrow. Maybe that skill will make all the difference in your family history.

Your siblings really can be your friends and not just kidney donors, but you can't take them, or their organs, for granted. If you find yourself resisting staying in touch, maybe work on that and figure it out. You will be happier with sibling pals in your life. For the rare sibling foe, well, you know how to change your phone number, right?

Parentification

It's a very well-established tendency to enslave children to do childcare. This is a problem, because slavery, but also because the enslaved are usually girls. Aside from the fact that this is obviously unfair, it is also tremendously convenient. Big sisters and brothers often enjoy swaddling babies and playing at parenthood; what could be more natural than insisting they do the childcare and do it without payment? You are already feeding them, hopefully. Why shouldn't they earn their keep?

Hey, it might be the only way the smaller kids get the nurture they need, in which case, hooray for sibling care! But if there's another way, maybe let the older kids have free time to be kids too. There are often laws about such things, and behind every law is some terrible story about a kid watching another kid watching another kid set a house on fire.

Although relatively rare, it must be mentioned, even if the older kid is qualified legally to take charge of other kids, the older kid may be evil. It happens. Well, maybe they are not actually evil, but they may be toying with some evil impulses, you know, the usual.

All this makes the babysitter selection more complex than some of us can handle. To make sure you have appointed them correctly: the supervisor kid must be old enough, competent, non-evil, and fairly compensated.

If you do enslave an older kid as a junior parent, understand that you are tweaking their sibling relationships and using your influence unfairly. Be sure to thank them for not being evil at the very least.

Daycare

Babysitters and daycare were a terrible problem for me, because I did not trust anyone to watch my kids when the kids were too young to tell me how their day went. Unless a baby has a really bad day, you will never notice.

My mother told me I had been kept in a playpen all day by one sitter because I didn't mind it. Another time, she said, she collected me covered in bite marks, which apparently, I also did not mind.

She may have told me some of these stories to persuade me to leave my kids with her, come to think of it. Huh. Either way, it worked. We had Gramma Care until we had chatty kids to report on the way it really went down.

Over the course of raising my kids, we did every type of daycare: stay at home, work at home, nanny at home, nanny away, Gramma's Mardi Gras, Daddy day care, pre-school co-op, church nursery, unemployed neighbor care, summer camp swim lesson torture, and nightmare rural day camp for one day only.

Only one injury occurred on someone else's watch, maybe two. Okay two. I think a near-miss stomach explosion counts as an injury. Those were both Gramma Mardi Gras problems. Wait, there were three. Somehow jumping off furniture at Gramma's house was a regular source of peril, along with the chance to eat your own weight in pastries.

So, it's probably best that Gramma retired very adamantly when kid three appeared on the scene. She knew that the third one gets your sanity and she hadn't enough sanity to spare.

I have listened to many moms and dads over the years stridently justify their choices about daycare and work balance and all I have to say is: calm down.

Some parents do serious damage by putting a huge priority on laser focused supervision. You know those parents by the way their kids cannot decide which shoe to put on first without direction.

Other parents take their inspiration from the sixties moms and only speak to the kids to tell them to shut up during their favorite daytime television shows.

Neither of these are good ideas.

If you are the heavy-duty supervision parent, maybe just a bit of outside daycare is going to save you all from spinning out in the washing machine of stay-at-home madness. You need to decide this for yourself. Nobody else can tell you what to do, until you get arrested for stealing and installing spy cams on the neighborhood squirrels or something.

We all start off with what is possible and go from there. People lectured me on how I had to get a job in order to pay someone to watch my kids. I nodded politely and didn't do that.

By the time you have three, you may only be able to get ahead by selling organs. Relax. Let the bills pile up for a while if they must until you figure out how to make it all work. Worry never pays the bills, even when it feels important.

When you have small children, it is something adjacent to impossible to make big professional leaps, and that's okay. If you can carve out time for your own education and still have a healthy relationship with your partner, congratulations! That must mean no one is ill for the time being.

There is no one answer and you will not be able to find the best arrangement if you are spending a lot of time being angry about the way you have boxed yourself in. It's a hard time, even for hard people.

Most people will not break your kids, but it is important to listen to your instincts. When you are evaluating a caregiver, ask yourself how they would handle really revolting situations. Would that teen drop your baby in the laundry if the going got gross? One babysitter I interviewed was clearly going through withdrawal, so I would also recommend not taking on a caregiver who clearly needs a caregiver of their own. Naturally, do not pay your babysitter in heroin.

Keep your antenna up for other options. One daycare is never enough. You have to be ready for your nanny to flee to Italy or your mom to quit 9 to 5 nurture. It happens. Things wash out like mountain roads in springtime.

Aside from the lack of exclusivity, daycare is a lot like marriage, you have to keep making the choice to stick with it. Every drop-off is a decision.

Interims

By the time you get expert at pumping yourself up with the sense that your daycare routine is a great method, it will be over. It's okay. You will find some other way to set all that money on fire.

Eventually, it will not feel strange or deranged to leave your kid with other people to witness their first adventure in snacking on bugs. In fact, you may have times when you believe the caregivers are simply better at caring for your kid than you are. You may imagine you want to be a truly professional parent.

Stop it. That's just your ovaries talking. You will never get out of daycare that way. If you suspect that you may become sentimental about the place, make friends there and stay in touch with them, elsewhere. If you continue to show up without kids, everyone is going to suspect you of something and they will be correct.

Sure, it feels like the expense and time involved will never end. The driving, the buckling, the bags of vegetables you didn't have time to chop, the parade of faces you struggle to name—it will come to an end, possibly with a sweaty ceremony and a sticky certificate. Yay, you!

Rivalry

Any kind of favoritism or scapegoating should be approached with extreme caution. Sure, it seems harmless if you occasionally say, "Why can't you be more like your sister?" It certainly seems to give the sister a big boost. Aside from the fact that it may be a sentence that is, unbeknownst to you, etched in a little brain for the rest of her life, it is also the way that systemic favoritism or scapegoating begins.

In little ways—a slightly longer turn, a skosh more attention and praise—you are sending messages to the offspring. They are paying much more attention than you are to such things, just ask them.

When you favor a child, you are doing them no favors. Aside from any added brattiness this favoritism may inspire, it also creates a focus for the irritation any of the other kids feel. There is now a reason they are treated unfairly, and that reason has a name. They can torment that reason in their spare time.

Shakespeare knew all about this and covered it a lot better than I can. Probably. The point is that those other kids will begin sharpening their metaphorical (and sometimes real!) knives over this treatment. You are setting the favorite up for a terrible fall.

One might think that scapegoating could be completely opposite and create a legacy of kindness for the scapegoated kid. In a way it might, but the scapegoated kid won't be able to enjoy it. If a little gal is continually chastised in front of the whole family, the others will not only feel sorry for her, but they will also begin to treasure her ability to pull the spotlight away from their own dirty deeds. She may hold a very dear spot in the family, but best case, she will have trouble trusting and connecting with people for a very long time. Worst case, she may embrace her bitterness and resolve to live up to her bad reputation.

Scapegoating can be a huge obstacle to stepparents. If the stepparents are unaware they are targeting some of the kids, they can really get rolling with it. They may build a case for doing exactly what they are doing and it's not great for everyone, including the parent.

Actively remembering your job is loving the kids helps avoid scapegoating, along with having another adult call bullshit on your bullshit.

As I mentioned, siblings need a chance to work things out. Certainly, intervene if they are chasing each other with hammers, but I recommend just taking away the hammers and letting the chasing go on. You are not the toy police or the argument police. Occasionally, you may need to be the judge, but be judicious about weighing into their situations.

Sometimes, distraction is your best tool.

"She called me a troglodyte!"

"How would you spell that?"

Pitting them against each other is the most destructive way to parent siblings, of course, and I am quite certain that if I had worked at it, I could have gotten someone maimed.

We had only one very memorable inquisition, at least that I can recall, and I have never stopped regretting it. A cookie disappeared and all six kids denied any knowledge of it. My inclination was to hide the cookies better until after dinner, but we ended up having an extended interrogation instead, or rather, the kids did.

They went about it methodically, motivated by the decree that no one would have another cookie until we got a confession. The older kids asked the younger kids questions, and there were cross-examinations. The four-year old's defense was a lack of height, and the nuances of the story made for a convincing tale. The eldest two (12 and 14) were terrible liars and were immediately disqualified by each other. The eleven-year-old, as I have mentioned previously, was in a tough spot, being at one of the least magical ages. On top of that, she had a previous record. The older kids were distracted during the questioning, as the seven-year-old faded into the woodwork of the basement den. She had a remarkable gift for this and nearly escaped consideration at all. One of the younger kids wasn't about to let her slide away, however, and pointed out that she could not make eye contact. They all closed in on her corner and we had a confession shortly thereafter.

Sure, the mystery was solved, but the cookie lie might as well have been a brand.

She carried that burden, bravely, for years.

Over time, I have watched many parents dig in and decide that a cookie battle is somehow a worthy hill of baked goods to die on. It's a matter of principle, it's an issue of trust, it's a commandment, dammit! But really, it is just a cookie. A cookie should start a conversation, not a war.

If you find yourself in a situation where there is clear favoritism, I think it's best for everyone to just accept it and overcome it with teamwork. If it's obvious that Daddy can never say no to little Pinto Bean, then clearly, she should be the one to suggest a side trip to the water park. Not that I ever encouraged such a strategy, of course. Water parks are full of germs.

If you can navigate the sibling sea without getting snared in the competitive current, or the guilty gusts, you can have a tremendous relationship to hang on to. Your siblings share your original tiny culture, if not your blood type. Even if they pranked you, ignored you or stole all your left shoes that one time, they understand some things about your early life that you may not. Ask them about it sometime.

Forgetting might be the only step you need to forgive the little slights. Forgiving systematic mistreatment and bullying is a whole process and it is enough work that a lot of people shy away and do easier things instead, like carve resentment totems. With their teeth.

As parents, we cannot engineer friendships between our kids. It may seem like we almost can manage their tastes and affections. It's a tantalizing mirage, but really, all we can do is demonstrate kindness, over and over and encourage their sparks of kindness for each other.

Chapter 4
The Mistake of Being Aloof

*It is well known that humor, more than anything else
in the human make-up, can afford an aloofness
and an ability to rise above any situation,
even if only for a few seconds.*
— Viktor E. Frankl

It's very much out of fashion in America now to be an aloof parent. Shipping kids away to school or lounging in your other trailer are rightly frowned upon. Sure, you may think you are fulfilling your calling, but don't forget the other calling that you have to the little spuds. They won't be little forever and they certainly won't be interested in you forever.

Whether you barricade yourself from your children with a demanding job, a gambling hobby or "writing a book" it's nearly the same effect to the kids. You are making yourself like Zeus.

Zeus

Zeus was a shitty parent. He abused his wife, who was also his sister, right in front of the kids. He threw various kids off his mountain, and he let Athena get away with everything. Even if his dad ate his kids, had bestiality problems, whatever, it's no excuse. Nothing could be as bad as Zeus abuse.

With that in mind, you may want to avoid putting yourself on a pedestal. Perhaps you are thinking, *But I don't think I'm a god! I don't even think I'm worthy of admiration! I'm mentally ill!* Okay. That's fine: you still need to make your crazy ass available to your kids. See, they don't know *what* your deal is and they really need to see it for themselves. Their default is to assume you are the greatest. You need to show them the reality of your less-than-greatness. Being a fake god is worse than being a god who is also a shitty parent.

Echoes

When I was allowed to volunteer at kindergarten, I saw what other parents might fear most: their kids telling on them to the teacher. While the teacher was giving a rote warning about the importance of seatbelts during safety week, one little boy's hand shot into the air with the confidence and wiggly desperation of a potty request. "My daddy doesn't need a seatbelt because he's super strong and the *govermint* can kiss his ass!"

The teacher nodded to me knowingly. She saw the lightbulb over my head. Whatever stupid slogans I had, and I had many, they were going to be repeated in the sharing circle. Things like, "If you break your sister's neck, you'll have to spoon feed her forever," and a favorite I stole from my friend, "We are not going to the emergency room today," all these were fodder for shockingly comprehensive toddler gossip.

You don't want to be reduced to the sum or your slogans, do you? If all your kids later remember is that you were prone to say, "During my time at Harvard…" you've really missed out.

Engaging

Tell them about the time you flunked out of Harvard, too; but more importantly, pay attention to their stories.

Being distant from your kids is like denying they are yours. There are going to be times you have your doubts—it happens to the worst of us. You may not want to go speculating that they may have been swapped out by the faeries, but you can totally read to them about other changelings and let them draw their own conclusions.

Maybe on the occasional Saturday you do feel a surge of regret for the simpler life you have forgotten. So, sure, get misty and then suck it up. Your life is cheerios and bedtime stories right now.

Evasion

I had a few terrible reveals to navigate with my kids. Cancer, divorce, and pet massacres are just the first to spring to mind. Any topic that makes you uncomfortable and any topic that may make them uncomfortable creates an extra special job for you.

It's tempting to skip the whole thing and let them make what they will of the empty chicken coop or hospital stay, but I do not recommend it. I avoided tough talks almost like a religion and it might keep things quiet, but it's an unclear quiet. The questions will probably pop up eventually, and it can get seriously weird, as can the questions.

Long after my divorce, one of my kids hesitantly approached me with her theory of why we split up the team. She really liked her theory, and I felt it was close enough to the truth to let her keep it. Her hesitance let me know how effectively I had shut down the discussion over time, so not my finest hour. Or year. Whatever.

Does a ten-year-old really need a comprehensive understanding of a pulverized romance? Probably not, but she did need to know that she didn't do anything wrong and she probably needed to feel like she could ask questions. Maybe in this instance getting it half right is as good as not getting it half wrong.

So, yeah, have the hard conversations, but have them at the kids' pace. "The chickens are all gone and I'm sad because I think something bad happened to them. What do you think?"

Making announcements and having no follow up can lead to kids being not only confused but frightened of their confusion. Sure, they can see or feel the moving van and the boxes, but there may be a bit more information they need to feel safe in this scenario.

It's certainly simpler to tell everyone big news at the same time, but if you have a pack of kids, there may be one who isn't really listening and they may only receive a garbled second-hand version of your description of radiation therapy.

Sometimes we avoid tough conversations because we fear the questions. It is perfectly natural and at the same time, fear of questions is no excuse. You can always respond to questions with thoughtful stalling, "I will have to think about that. Let's talk again tomorrow." You are also allowed to take a break for your own overwhelmed emotions if you need it. "I'm going to wash my face and feet and come back in a few minutes. I might also wash the dog."

If they have strong emotions in response to your news, you may imagine it will be unbearable. This can be funny in retrospect because we nearly always bear the unbearable. We bear and we bear again. Ugh. So much bearing. Even if you are barely bearing, you are still bearing it.

Don't try to dodge by telling kids they should not have whatever feelings you don't want to acknowledge. You're not here to pick their emotions for them, remember? You don't have to rush everyone back into the feeling better bus, just make sure no one gets left behind.

Intermissions

That's not to say that you should never be aloof for an instant. Plan on it and limit it. Don't take an unplanned break from parenthood for a few years, unless you are obliged to do so by a pesky law or something. Definitely do take time for yourself to do other things, as long as one of those other things is not restricted to sitting around with other parents complaining about parenting.

Lots of people get so engrossed in parenting that they burn themselves out and then essentially quit. This is only a good thing for those Zeus-persons. If they quit being bad dads, that's bound to be a general plus column event. For the rest of us, it's important to pay attention to things other than parenting, even when it feels like there are no other things.

Take a class on baking, but not "Baking for Baby." Study a foreign language or visit an art museum where kids aren't allowed. This sort of vacation is vital to you and to your little jerks. You might take this time to get reacquainted with your partner so that you snap out of thinking of them as the Second Shift or Crewmate Spud; talking about the kids during these times should be off limits, naturally.

Your breaks should be outside you and outside your parenting life. They don't have to be expensive. Hike, borrow a kayak from the neighbors who like that sort of thing, or hunker down at the library with a stiff cup of coffee and a book that plants your brain in another body.

Visiting your therapist doesn't count as a break, that's simply brilliant brain maintenance. Naturally of all the things you may be tempted to neglect, don't leave your brain laying around to rust. Keep it humming on the healthiest frequency you can manage. It will thank you by saving you a lot of avoidable trouble.

Commanding

If you are wrapped up in your own nervous breakdown, you might miss the first signs of the ones the kids are having. You have to be there and be aware, there's no substitute or stepparent that can do it for you. Only you can parent your way, see it your way and get out of their way.

If you're always giving instructions and dictating adjustments, you're still Zeusing out on your kids. Haven't you seen the kid who blinks hard and tries again with the added pressure of his dad's gaze? Each fix-it impulse that turns into a command sends a message that there is something wrong with the kids. It separates you from them very effectively with a slice of judgement in between.

I mean, it's fine to teach them things, that's part of the job, but it's still only part of the job. There's the heartbeat when you don't say anything and look at them with a face that asks, "Now what?"

If you have all the answers, they will stop asking questions and eventually you'll end up barking orders at people who aren't even certain you belong at their yard sale.

Then again, you could always start a blog and fill it with your wisdom and watch how hard your kids will not read it.

Orientation

So, once you've realized that you've been aloof and missed so many ways to be connected to your kids, relax. You're still here and they have grown very independent in the meantime. They have done their own laundry and only tried to put the cat in the dryer that one time you noticed. They don't expect people to magically slip a plate under their crumbs and they have an assortment of people to support them in different ways.

You may recognize with a pang that they have another parent stand-in, but there's no way she's the one they'll call when they need dental surgery. You're still number one for the hard stuff, I bet!

Be aware that you will not always like your kids and they will not always like you. It's fine. Maybe they dislike the way you get drunk and argue with lawn furniture. Maybe they're right. Maybe you shouldn't hide away in a fog of substances quite so much. You could wait to dive into the liquor until you are eighty and the survival of your liver is truly optional.

Be there. Be awake. It's over before you know it.

Chapter 5
The Mistake of Being Terrible at Marriage

*Everybody in the world is thinking: I wish there was
just one other person I could really talk to,
who could really understand me,
who'd be kind to me.*
—Doris Lessing

Frequently, when talking to young folks about their budding romance, or fresh nuptials, I must stop myself mid-suggestion. I am not good at marriage, so they should not listen to me about that stuff.

In those moments, I stop, make a disconcerting series of rewind sounds, and then I offer to be a sympathetic ear for any situation on the cusp of a serious error. I can spare them some trouble, having made all the mistakes I can conjure to mind.

I could list them here, but I won't. If you find my marriage chatter too depressing, by all means, skip ahead to the divorce section. It's much more chipper.

For all my marriage-like arrangements, I was only married one time during the first 30 years of being a parent. It's fine. Honestly, no one ever truly wanted to marry me, not even that one guy who did. Sure, like any young female, I had random marriage proposals at

diners and laundromats, but no one has ever seriously
wanted to marry me.

How did it all get so out of hand if no one wanted to
say, "I do"? I have decided it's my own refusal to say, "I
don't." By golly, I was going to have an adoring spouse
and a pack of children because I wanted what I wanted.
When your precious plans hinge on other people
bending to your will, you really should just sit down and
give your strategy another think.

It is not self-deprecation to point out how completely
no one actually wanted to marry me; it's intended to be
encouraging! If no one wants to marry you, maybe you
shouldn't force the issue. Maybe you could cultivate
enjoying your own company and use your tremendous
resolve on yourself instead of badgering some
unfortunate mate to wash your car.

You can try to tell other people this, that they
should just quit trying to get hitched. They will never
thank you, I have learned, and they may ban you from
their internet rodeo for trying to "educate" them.

When you choose to embrace the fact that no one
wants to commit, you have a great many options. You
can decide not to have a committed arrangement, or
perhaps develop a clutch of friends for various arenas of
your life. Maybe all you really need is friends who will
ride trains to museums and a few other friends who will
talk you out of ice skating and will talk you into
mammograms.

It sounds like a lot of work to build a tribe, but every
option is a lot of work. Being alone is a lot of work too.
It's also a lot of work to bully a series of people to put up
with you and help you pay the rent.

Staffed

There is an upside to a lot of family heaving and cleaving. We don't hear about the stepparents who work out, but most of them do. It turns out that three parents for four kids who only had two, and two parents for two kids who only had one; well, more parents can be a pretty big advantage, even if one of them is a disaster magnet. Maybe that should read *"especially* when one is a disaster magnet."

When one kid needed braces for her teeth, we could find a way to pay for them, and when another kid had a field trip, she always had somebody who could take time off work.

No one parent is going to have all the forms of expertise needed for every situation. The real world is far too complicated and becoming an expert on one thing means passing up expertise in something else. One person cannot even be an expert on parenting, no matter how spiffy their search engine. We have to recognize who has the most patience for kid movies, and who can keep a clean-up crew focused and mildly miserable for an afternoon. If they need a perfect, shiny excuse, I'm on it. That's just my area.

Singles

During the year and a half when I had four kids on my own, I was fending off panic attacks as I realized, bit by bit, there was no way I could manage the situation and provide for them. Nope nope nope. One kid had to have a science project done and another kid needed trumpet accessories and what was the smell in the hallway about anyway?

I disconnected the television so the kids would learn crafts and music. We went out to play in freezing weather and swam through heat advisories, as if fresh air was going to give us fresh ideas.

It became a kind of retreat or intermission, if it's possible to have such a thing with a bunch of young children. I let the housework take care of itself, which it really never does. My lack of concentration and general madness made for poor employment options and I got suckered into a contracting job that required I pay for stuff to do the job. At least I learned another way not to not break even.

Anyhoo, in the evenings, we went to the playground and lolled with other families like mountain villagers. It was beautiful. We had nothing in common and everything in common; proximity, weariness, and a drive to do right by our kids. One mail-order wife, a stiffed heiress, a child bride, a teacher, and the multi-job moms we didn't see very often; all those moms still have a special mom-shaped spot in my heart.

We didn't bash men, in fact, we didn't need to since we thought we knew what we were doing, despite the multiple divorces we represented. When a husband misbehaved, the rest of us exchanged significant glances. We knew what he was doing, even if we truly did not.

Some of us were just having a sabbatical from home ownership, a little pause between bigger phases. Others of us were contemplating a downward spiral each time there was a bad turn. I was one of those, and the other moms kept an eye on me, kindly. The only moms who were genuinely spiraling were doing it with the help of drugs. Whether their drugs were medical or illicit, it made no difference to the void.

Anyone who wanted to date was dating, but dating had changed.

In midlife, we were no longer the center of a field of suitors. How rude. Instead, we were assessed by men of means and discarded by rumpled suits with hair plugs. They were wary of us because we might be insane.

I learned to be very efficient. Instead of having a series of dinners to get to the question of future plans, if someone presented themselves as a serious boyfriend candidate, I led with, "I have four kids." Silence was the typical reaction—ghostly radio silence, and on to the next fish in the sea.

Online dating was effective and infuriating. Why would people go to the trouble of navigating intricate matchmaking mazes only to lie, or complain about their exes, or claim they aren't looking for matches as much as the making part. What?

Determined to cancel my most expensive and exasperating dating subscription, I checked in one more time to shut it down when I saw I had a blinky notification signifying a new pal with potential.

"What number of kids is your ideal?" was my favorite of the canned questions.

"As many as I can support," was the shocking reply from my last guy.

I wished so hard for a man to show up who would be the damned CEO of my life and let me get some sleep, and there he was.

When that happened, it was really lucky, but also another dreadful deal in its own way. For someone who is terrible at marriage to embark on another pseudo marriage—when power struggles were also a member of the family—was a questionable choice, but, hey, the kids were all for it!

Because we realized that the kids were counting on this arrangement, we kept at it, even as a therapist weighed in to say we might not have a healthy collaboration style. I used to think therapists didn't say things like that, but I'd heard the same thing three different times. Diagnosis: I am the asshole, also.

Blaming

This is the key to having a bad marriage: be ultra-vigilant in pointing the finger elsewhere. Lament at length about how you cannot find your soulmate without taking a moment to wonder if there's a problem with your own soul.

Remember: they did this to you. You cannot change them and you cannot accept them, so sit permanently between those problems and complain about your shitty relationship bookends. This exercise will guarantee as many bad marriages as you will need in order to be convinced: partnership is not for you.

I could have been so much better as a partner if I had recognized that I had a long way to go, instead of working so hard on attacking their foibles. I'm sorry about the torches and the endless phone conversations about how horrible they were for making me feel horrible. It was all about my baggage and its poor chemistry with their baggage. Classic.

During a break-up, some people will behave as if they need to solve the mystery of what went wrong. It's like they had no warning that you would leave if they didn't quit secretly drinking too much and being a big old fascist.

What could possibly be the problem?

I don't even blame myself any longer. Sure, it sounds like it, but it's not blame. I am responsible for my choices and they were sometimes very, very poor choices, but there's no time machine in my pocket to go back and revise any of it. I made my bed. Figuratively, of course.

Now, I believe that it could never have been any easier. It certainly could have been so much worse. I am often grateful for an ordinary level of unhappiness.

Options

Not everyone is meant for marriage and not every marriage is meant to be crawling with kids. You have choices and things change even when you don't change them on purpose. *Cest la vie, mofo.*

Maybe try something else, like burnishing your own mental and emotional health. Your partner might still be around, a bit slumped and discouraged but patient. People have fixed worse problems than your marriage and people have been more appalling people than you are. As you get better, you will be one of the better people too.

I would venture that most every couple considers splitting up or divorcing at some point. As we trudge through the roughest patches, it's hard on a partnership—any partnership.

We had vacations during which every single person acquired a stomach bug. Not only was there the general suffering and disgust of the operation, but every single relationship suffered too. Some of us wanted to be pitied more than others, some of us hogged the resources, and some of us had a scorched earth policy. Sometimes there were an insufficient number of toilets for events.

Couple and family life is hard even when there aren't dueling health problems, massive infidelity or a slipping mask of sanity. Just keep in mind that once you have kids, if you split up you will be dealing with each other for many years to come. So, he got the babysitter pregnant? Bummer. He's still your problem too. I'm sorry. I didn't invent marriage and divorce; I've just done them all wrong.

Ending

There is a tendency to burrow into a bad relationship, even when the odds of success are continually dimming. Maybe that's only a problem for the optimists, but even for the happy ending non-believers, our beloved pessimists, the pull to stay is extraordinarily strong.

The fallacy of sunk costs suggests that we get stuck on the investment we have already made in the relationship. When you have worked so hard at being able to scold with only a snort or if you have perfected your ability to avoid the Saturday night fights, it's very difficult to unwind all of it for something new. Victimhood is miserable, but even that sort of misery becomes home base over time, especially if you hang up your ancestral curtains and really give it your all.

Other times, if the situation is less dire, you may get bogged down in imagining the other person moving on without you. You squint and you can almost see them traipsing, because in this fantasy they are showered with good fortune and have tons to traipse about.

Don't fall for it. Everybody has to grapple to earn their traipsing times. They can't be happier without you, unless you leave, you think. No, you think wrong: they will almost certainly be the same amount of happy in short order, because that's how happiness works.

Their future happiness is none of your business, anyway, if you are paying proper attention to your own.

In my view of relationships, you are always deciding if you are heading in or heading out. Each time you are cruel, you are pushing people away. Each little pinch of ridicule adds to the recipe of divorce.

Pros and cons may not balance out if you have a distorted view of your relationship, but when the real deal is out of whack, everyone knows. If you are not actively adding to the "pro" side, you know it. You are opting out right there in front of yourself.

Your kids see the whole picture, and they will have front row seats to the breakup. Sure, you can try to keep secrets, but they will know something is rotten in

Denmark[7] Kids may be confused about the nature of the
rottenness, and they always have the option to decide
it's you.

Divorcing

Divorces happen every day, but they don't have to
be the worst outcome. Regardless of most issues, you
can *be excellent to each other.*

This requires that you both (or all) get over being
angry and blaming each other for the end of the
marriage. Blame is comfortable, but blame never feels as
good as having your kids feel comfortable with the end
of your marriage. That is so hard and so worth doing,
you will turn in circles patting yourself on the back if
you can manage it.

It is possible to *not talk shit* about your ex to your
kids for fifty years. I have witnessed this miracle
personally. If your would-be ex is an irredeemable waste
of oxygen, trust your kids to figure that out for
themselves. You don't have to tell them not to loan her
money. You don't have to be the one to spoil the
surprise on his secret life as a harmless degenerate.

Keeping as much harmony as possible is your top
priority in a divorce. It might seem like the top priority is
the property division or the reputation problems or the
cat collection. Nope. None of that will matter as much to

---

[7] Mentioning corruption in Denmark is an overused
reference to a play called "Hamlet" in which people choose
murder over divorce. Do not try this at home. Murder is far
too permanent and lazy. Oh, you don't think Hamlet's mom
was a murderer? Cute!

you as your kids' peace of mind. Make sure they know that none of it is their fault and if you don't believe that, get busy believing it so you can sell it all day long.

Kids, possibly all kids, naturally assume disasters are personal and they assume it's their fault when something painful happens. Adults know better, but the kids really don't know it's not their fault, and worse they can interpret their personal disasters in very painful ways. They may conclude they don't deserve love, care or safety. It's up to us to show them this is not true.

No kid deserves to see their favorite people go their separate ways—not even the worst kid. Of course, all kids are amazing and wonderful, but there has to be one who is the actual worst kid. Don't worry; it's probably not you.

Dangerous

Some situations cannot be truly or artificially harmonious. As long as the ex is dangerous, you cannot safely dabble with harmony.

Is he dangerous? Not sure? Ask a meter maid, a psychiatrist, a lawyer, and your gut. If your gut is telling you he's dangerous, the gut gets at least two votes.

A violent ex needs to be blocked in every way. No notes or phone calls. No texts or brief visits. You may feel tempted to dip back into the pool of tasty, tasty drama from time to time, because people have bizarre urges that go completely against their self-preservation. Don't fool yourself into juggling rattlesnakes, and keep your eyes wide open for that sort of temptation.

Anyone who interferes with your decisive placement of that person in the metaphorical hazardous waste dump is putting themselves in jeopardy of exile too. By that I mean, if you have friends or relatives who keep in contact with an ex you have blocked, you may have to block them too. Safety first, especially with vicious crumbs.

If you are in a violent relationship, people will help you escape and most won't even say "I told you so." Get help and get the kids out. They are your top priority now that you made them.

When I was living with my former partner, better known as My Favorite Maniac, I spend an inordinate amount of time trying to get him diagnosed with something so that I could figure out what to do. If it was only alcoholism, as I first thought, the fix is relatively simple—not easy but simple.

It was not simple. Substance abuse is just the top of the carrot once people reach 35 or so. It's usually their way of avoiding dealing with other pain, like insecurity, fear of failure, or general madness. Some people who abuse chemicals are working hard at *borking* up their lives and the rest of their carrot is pure disaster.

When they begin destroying furniture because they dislike the dinner menu, it's time to go. Naturally, this is just my educated opinion on that type of carrot of craziness.

Even if the kids don't experience violence first hand, being around it is harmful. They are super-resilient, but why not let them use that resilience for bouncing back from unavoidable sorrow instead of the avoidable kind.

Don't get casual with the kids' ability to bounce back. The fact that they can take it is a terrible excuse for letting needless trauma unfold.

They may need their resilience for the time their grandmother dies skydiving or when some kid at school gets creepy and punches them in the kisser. It's best to protect that resilience as you would a finite supply of precious puppies.

So, by all means, go ahead and divorce if nothing else will work, but it bears repeating: if you share kids, your ex will be in your life, even if only in the margins. Make sure you only marry someone you are enthusiastic about having as an ex, too.

If, when you are first getting acquainted, they are intimidating or they ask you to help them screw over their previous partner, perhaps take a pause. Maybe give that situation more than a minute's consideration. Anybody who trashes their previous partners will do it to you too, maybe while you are standing right there, holding their sperm sample.

If you must make a baby, please be selective with your baby makers. If you rely on that birth control you forgot to use, you too can end up having to tell a kid their dad was a maniac. Nobody expects maniacs.

Chapter 6
The Mistake of Not Maintaining Friendships

Regard one who sees your faults as a guide to a
hidden treasure. Stay close to one so wise
and astute who corrects you
when you need it.
– Buddha

Once you have a kid, all your relationships shift sideways. Nobody else matters in quite the same way, but if you really think that, you're wrong. The other people in your life didn't stop being who they are, you just stopped making time for them.

Upkeep

Your friends don't have to be parents, because it doesn't matter if they "get you" in one particular slice of your life. I fell into that weird pseudo-elitist mindset with friends who didn't share my lifestyle or my deathstyle; they were going to have to be cut from the team.

It was too hard to try to care about their pre-child complaints. Did they get a full night's sleep this year?

Pfft to them. Oh, how cute, the way they worried about wedding plans or jobs or car loans. Try worrying about a tiny human choking on its own tiny teeth and get back to me. Their horror could not compete with my horror.

This is completely wrong, of course. Just because it's harder to connect with your friends, that doesn't mean you quit. Friendship is not supposed to be easy and breezy all the time. So what if you forgot if her new husband is Greg or Gary; pick one and get on with the conversation. Nobody cares! Not even Gary or Greg.

Terrible

I was a terrible friend. Because I didn't learn better for a very long time, I thought that friends were people you entertained with your complaints. Much like some shitty television friend who appeared only to rant and steal some crackers from their pal, I was something worse than useless.

Gradually I got the idea that friends were too much work unless they were perfect friends and you know what? There are no perfect friends. They are going to have problems at inconvenient times and they are going to annoy you with their stories about their other friends who you suspect are better at most things than you will ever be. On top of all that, at the worst possibly moment, they will remind you of the time of your greatest humiliation at the swimming pool.

Endurance

That's the point of having friends. It's not a revolving door of auditions and unreturned messages, it's having people around you who you mostly trust and who have known you long enough to call bullshit on your bullshit. Who you were is never going to be more important than who you are, but they have the context. You can appreciate each other's journey like no one else.

I didn't like the bullshit aspect. I wanted friends who only saw the mostly functioning, mostly happy version of me. That is beyond misguided and supremely shallow.

One of the beauties of creating your own deeply embarrassing and flawed life is that you must release your illusions. You cannot expect anyone else to hang onto your illusions either, unless you want to be really rude.

Neighbors

I have lost track of nearly all our old neighbors; social media keeps a couple of delicate connections distantly thrumming, but that's all.

My newer friends, the ones who have not moved in decades, enjoy talking about their deep connections, and diapering one another's kids, and staying close through neighborhood infidelities, weather disasters and weapons charges.

These stories pain me—no exaggeration, they give me a physical pain. It's exactly the way you feel when you eat a taco too quickly, sense that it is somehow sideways, and then realize you will just politely suffocate right there in the summertime drive thru.

That feeling might be called envy, but I now know it as regret. If we hadn't moved so many times, we'd have those kind of neighbors, wouldn't we? No, probably not.

I know people who are experts at keeping connections, and moving is just a minor inconvenience. They gather with their old summer camp friends, their reality show pals, whatever. Meanwhile, I can't clearly recall the names of the people I hung out with last year.

Priorities will bite you, right on the ass, given enough time and momentum.

Your friends are not just there for your complaints or to give you emergency bone marrow. Help with organ emergencies is nothing to sneeze at, but there are plenty of other considerations. It's good for you to resist chasing off everyone over every minor slight, I bet. Being open to their weird ideas, at least enough to listen to them, is nourishing. It's good for us in a way that just watching people's stories cannot replicate.

Unloading your minor irritations and withholding your deepest fears is a guaranteed way to avoid fostering real friendships. Not telling people you have a terrible disease will keep you isolated, and it will help them feel that you didn't value their support when they find out you were ill. I have test driven this mistake personally, and it works with outstanding efficiency in alienating potential new friends and old ones.

Having long-time friends is important in hard times, but it can be even more important when your circumstances are looking up; for instance, if you become wildly rich your long-time friends become crucial. You still can't trust anyone to genuinely like you, but at least you have a chance with your oldest pals. They have already put up with you this long, so they aren't likely to murder you for your scratch-off winnings now.

Moving

It's generally accepted that we should pick a place to settle down and raise kids instead of traipsing around every few years and uprooting them. Ahem. Some parents have to relocate for work, but if your calling is a travelling circus, parenthood particularly may not be a good idea.

Each time we moved, it seemed necessary, although in retrospect I see that it was just an obscure symptom of pregnancy. The first time, we suddenly needed to live somewhere without lead paint. I could have tested the house we had for lead, but I thought it logical to just move everything when I wasn't supposed to lift anything. I didn't test the new house for lead either, but I felt safer about it. Ironically, the fact that I behaved this way, may actually be tied to my own lead exposure, not from paint but from being born in the 1960s when lead was in the air and in all the playground equipment.

We moved again when I was pregnant again. The logic was pure simplicity; we needed to keep my grandmother's house available for her. It turns out that the rest of the family was unhappy with this burst of bad logic and elected to sell the house we were in. This necessitated another move during the third pregnancy, which led to a whole series of moves.

So, moving when you are pregnant is crazy. Do it every time if you really, really want to make everything worse with your emotional reasoning and to generate a fog of strain.

The many moves also meant that none of us kept any friendships for very long. Every three years is still about the time I start to feel like firing my friends, regardless of anything they may or may not have done in the interim.
Similarly, every three years I am pushing for some sort of divorce from whoever is around. After all these cycles, I now recognize it's just an alienation rhythm, like a huge insect popping out of the ground to eat everything in its path, breed and die.

Later

It is possible to continue to make friends, but you have to be willing to stick your friendly neck out. When little kids make friends, they just declare their friendship, one step, no fuss. Older people struggle more because they expect a fuss. They expect rejection or they worry the new friend will steal all their dimes.

It is tempting to give up after one person doesn't respond according to your expectations. That stings, why do it again? You need to do it again, and again because you are showing your kids how to get out there an embrace the world.

Are you superstitious that all your friendly attempts cause everyone bad luck? Get over yourself. Bad luck happens and it's not up to you, you weirdo.

Most other people are not great at making and being friends either! It's not just you. Cut yourself some slack, then cut them some slack and keep trying. I don't recommend you keep trying with the same standoffish friend candidate, unless you want to be a stalker. Ask new people as often as you can stand, "Let's be friends, okay?" just like you did when you were five years old.

Generosity

Hopefully, like me, your kids are better at friend stuff. I marvel at how my kids navigate friendships. They have considerate strategies for letting everyone feel loved. I have no idea how that happened.

The more bashful kids have the hardest time with friendships. They pre-decide that fuss is going to result from friendly overtures. They are afflicted with so much worry about what they are causing others to think, they cannot get out of their own way at times. Starting from a well of self-consciousness makes the whole ordeal even more of an ordeal. You need emotional ladders and compasses and imaginary pudding to keep your imaginary strength up. It's a lot.

I always have advised them to adjust their focus outward in those situations. When they have a flare up of shyness, find someone who is even more shy and try to help them out. Occasionally, the more shy person is insane, but at least you learned something instead of hanging back and learning from afar the entire time.

Some of the kids put all their eggs in one egg, or something, and I'm sure that's my fault. You can have more than one best friend, I say, and they cheerfully ignore me. Friends are hard work and best friends can be the best work, but you don't want the exclusivity to be a source of pressure, I bet.

Whatever your friend-style, or lack thereof, your kids will learn things about how to nurture or neglect friends from you. If you don't teach them that friends are not usually people who drain you and carry on about coupon guilt, they may have to figure that out for themselves. If you don't show them how to avoid ghosting when ghosting[8] has all the appeal, they may become habitual ghosters when every day is Halloween.

When you observe your kids making terrible friends, you have a couple of choices. You can maneuver to expose the terribleness of the friends in short order, but that's very difficult if you have a job or other kids to wrangle. Are you some kind of maniacal movie matriarch? Is this how you finally find out? It's probably easier to wait it out and trust the kids to discover the terrible nature of their pals.

Then again, you could just pack up and move.

------

[8] Ghosting is a newer term for rudely ignoring a person who has failed to perfectly fulfill your expectations. Sometimes rudeness is the perfect way to fulfill their expectations, but not in most cases.

Chapter 7
The Mistake of Being Immature

I always wanted to be somebody, but now I realize I should have been more specific.
– Lily Tomlin

The idea of bluffing your way through situations has a lot of appeal, but it's really going to wreck your parenting game. If you indulge in hypocrisy or just mimic what your parents did, or try to ape what you think your favorite musician is like with her kids it's not going to work out.

Faking

Being authentic in your parenting isn't just a concept, it's a requirement. If you don't understand what that means, take some time to figure it out. Going through the motions isn't good enough. Would you appreciate being parented by a sleepwalker or a robot? Okay, granted that might be an improvement for some of us, but if you had the choice between an automatic and thoughtless parent and having a couple of adults who were real and really human with you, I have to believe you'd opt for the real human team.

Be as honest as you can stand with kids. Say "I don't know" instead of "Nobody knows." The sooner your kids get used to the idea that we're all in this stupid carnival together, the better.

You might think that rubbing your chin and grunting as if there is some higher understanding you can't quite impart to their tiny minds is great, but it's also the worst. It is not reassuring for them to think you know things that you won't share.

By the same token, don't overshare, for heaven's sake. Don't tell them answers to questions they haven't asked.

As an example, when they ask you what a penis is for, don't say you don't know. If they are pretty young, it's fine to let them know there's some debate about what a penis is for, but mostly it's for peeing in any direction. Some details can wait and other details are simply not ready for you to trot out and invite to dinner.

One of my gals wanted to know all about penises and was really angry that she couldn't figure out how to pee like a boy. Sometimes there's no right way to give answers to kids like her. Some kids have to take all kinds of time to get acquainted with facts and they will not accept your version of anything with simplicity.

She was on a collision course with toilets that could not be prevented. I must admit I am not completely certain that she didn't solve the stand-up urination problem. Maybe she did. All I know is that the days of finding the evidence of her training stopped, and that was all I really required.

People like to say that boys are easier, and in this particular situation, they are. All we have to do is provide a target and a little encouragement and keep the cleaning supplies nearby. Bonus points if you can help them feel comfortable with just sitting down and removing all the drama from the exercise.

Spanking

Other parents love to tell you what they think of your choices and they love to mock you. This is not your problem, it's their insecurity and embarrassment about their own weird ways. Dads who cross their arms to say, "Spare the rod and spoil the child," probably mean well, but they are essentially telling you to beat your kids. They really believe that some kids require smacking, so you need to think about what you really believe before you accept their advice.

Nearly half the people I have ever discussed parenting with have insisted that spanking is useful for stubborn kids. That half of mankind is 100% wrong on that. There's good research[9] that establishes how wrong they are. Nonetheless, I'm not going to bully you with

---

[9] Gershoff, E. T., & Grogan-Kaylor, A. (2016). Spanking and child outcomes: Old controversies and new meta-analyses. *Journal of Family Psychology, 30*(4), 453–469. A good explanation of the meta-analyses was published by the University of Texas at the time. https://news.utexas.edu/2016/04/25/risks-of-harm-from-spanking-confirmed-by-researchers/. As to what a meta analysis is, well, you are smart, but I'll tell you to save the search—it's a study of all the available data and if it's done well, it considers all the bias and defects of that data to give a clear, big picture. So now we know spanking is bad news, overall. We also have established that I can make a very serious footnote, overall.

facts when I can sprinkle my own personal experience on top.

I tried the spanking idea when I had run out of other ideas and reached a desperate impasse. Since we had moved into a house that was attached to a shop full of deadly machinery, a significant safety problem developed. I was required to keep everyone in bed at bedtime and my usual eye roll at the late requests for water was not enough. With no time to address the hyped-up anxiety they were experiencing that made them want to run around and explore at night, serious action was required. If they did run around at night, they could literally be maimed by heavy equipment.

Everybody cried about the spanking and it solved nothing. Outrunning me became a priority that week, so there could have been an unintended upside if I created a track star.

I did not create a track star.

It made a big impression and they still remember the spanking. They do not remember the threat of spanking or the way I stuck to my guns or what they did to get in that much trouble, because none of that was shocking. That anyone they trusted would snap and hit them on purpose was the surprise, and somehow it did not improve anything.

It was a huge waste of tears. On top of that they still did not fear me, so I felt doubly robbed.

Transparency

It's important to be open about your regrets. When things go wrong, kids need to see the aftermath and the cleanup, too. This is much like my view of arguing. You may argue in front of the kids on occasion, but be certain to make peace in front of them too. They'll never understand how apologies work on the sophisticated level of saying more than, "I'm sorry you were offended," if they don't see a semi-pro at work.

You can demonstrate your decision-making process, even if it's less of a process and more of a series of loopy conversations with yourself. If you are going to try something drastic and bonkers that affects the whole family, be ready to explain a really good reason. "What the hell," is not one of those reasons.

What makes a good reason? Well, you have to know in your bones, or have an instinct that is true to your deepest beliefs, an inspiration that is so authentic you want to get a tattoo of it. On your face. Even with all that commitment, your brilliant scheme still might be wrong.

How can you know your brilliant scheme is less than brilliant? Where does it come from? Is it from fear? An idea like, "I will move my entire family onto a cult ranch so that we won't have any more burglaries," is such a plan. You really need to look at this from some other angles. What is the sacrifice here? Sure, your local family sucks, but the Manson family sucks more. Maybe just skip Thanksgiving and get a big dog. Smaller adjustments have smaller catastrophes attached to them. Usually. Whatever your cunning plans, be as open as possible with the kids. Sometimes their observations are much more salient than those of any adult who is tangled up in rational yarn.

Identity

Where do these brilliant schemes come from? Are they your own, really? Who the heck are you anyway? You might want to figure out what sort of person you are before you start forming more persons.

I didn't do it that way. I believed I was a kind and truthful person but I didn't understand that it was possible to be like that and to be really angry and dishonest at the same time.

As a teen, if anyone asked me who I really was, I would freeze. I always hated that sort of question. At the end of the *Wizard of Oz* movie I would sweat for Dorothy. "What have you learned, Dorothy?" *Gah.* Are we really supposed to be learning and explaining ourselves all the time?

Who was I? I was a chameleon who would reflect some boyfriend's expectations back very skillfully to hide whatever was really boiling in my brain. I was probably thinking about how much I envied him his confidence and even admiring his arrogance. If he wasn't kind, it was probably because I didn't deserve kindness. What a crazy baby.

If you are starting out from a home base of irrationality and narcissism, you have a long journey to the mental health needed to parent yourself and other people, believe me. But you know what? You will never get there if you don't take some steps, even very small steps. Very slight course corrections can make a huge difference later. Every time you solve a little error in your thinking, you build up a repertoire of better solutions for the future.

If you start the journey from a peak of clarity and harmony, that peak is probably an illusion, so enjoy the scenery while you fall down and then get real.

Figure out what you value, truly. If you look at the way you spend your time, maybe your highest priority is video games. Are you sure that's where you want to put your hours? You may need those reflexes for a few other things. A spare life isn't going to *boop* up for you in the end of your real life. [10]

If you aren't sure about your priorities, maybe ask other people what they think. It should be people who know you, not some hot bartender or someone else expecting a tip.

Very squeamishly now, I remember asking the kids what their favorite things were and what they thought my favorite things were. Without hesitation, one kid said, "Your no-no things." It was the worst answer she could have given and it was totally true from a kid's eye view. My no-no things were always nearby and I tracked them like the addict I was, because my no-nos were full of deliciously vital nicotine.

The horror of learning that my young children believed that my drug was my top priority was the beginning of the end of my habit. It didn't belong with

---

[10] It has been pointed out that I may criticize video games excessively. That's nice. It's a personal grudge, so I will allow it. You might substitute in any other excessive diversion distracting you from your deep goals.

us any more than a bad case of lice. It was an interloper that wasn't welcomed in our next new life.

*

You really are somebody, you know. Don't take parenting as an opportunity to hide out in all the busy work and trappings of parenting instead of figuring out who you are and who you can be. Really. Trust me on this, assuming you can trust me on anything in here. If you don't take an interest in who you are on your own, your empty nest is going to be a thing of dread. If you know who you want to be without soccer games and school plays, your next phase could actually be exciting. As the kids need less bandwidth, maybe you can start a band! Or a grow-your-own weird tomato farm. I don't know what your enthusiasm can create, but you can know, so find out!

Goals

If you are honest with yourself and have a clear concept of the person you want to be that's a great start. I don't mean the person that you want to appear to be. Don't ruin some portrait in your attic.[11] If we could transfer the effort we put into appearing to be smart into actually learning things, we would already be super smart.

---

[11] This is me pretending to be clever by referencing an oft-referenced book that is largely unreadable and extremely preachy, "The Picture of Dorian Gray."

Perhaps, periodically contemplate Future You and check your progress. You'll usually find progress if you are trying at all.

If you want to be a patient, healthy grandmother, maybe learn how to quit yelling and exercise a bit more. If you want to have a pack of friends to run into the ocean with, maybe get out of the house and meet some people who like the same things, such as oceans.

You know who you meet in your own house? Paramedics!

If you want to be the cool mom, you need to first recognize that there is no way to be that person intentionally. Nothing is less cool that a mom trying to be cool. One kid likes to tell me when I veer into behavior that she calls "White Lady Trying Too Hard." That is not cool. When I point out, testily, that we are not, strictly speaking, 100% white, that is also not cool.

Maybe come up with a short list of specific traits instead of striving for coolness. Do you want to be trustworthy, hard-working, respectable, affectionate, kind, patient? Great! Those are really good attributes of a parent. Do you want to be impulsive, irrational, unbound by time, pitiable, selfish, cranky-ass? Also great! Get some fish instead of kids.

You don't have to be perfectly formed and situated before you have kids. It rarely goes that way, anyhow. You do need to put in the work to become the person you want to be, in order to mold the people you want to have in your home on a regular basis.

You can do those things at the same time, because humans are great at renewing themselves. We have to be great at fixing ourselves, since we're so good at breaking ourselves.

Truthfulness

While I was an immature parent, I did have a fetish for the truth. Very few people I have ever met are more screwy with the truth, and yes, that outfit makes you look lumpy.

During a mandatory bout of my own teen therapy, I gained a nugget of perception that has been the foundation for my shaky house of mental health ever since.

My therapist, named Rob, as are all therapists, jumped up during one of my painful monologues and began to draw on the white board. He had what I now know was an epiphany. This is another reason all therapists are named Rob; people named Rob have the most epiphanies.

Rob knew how to persuade me to be more honest by appealing to my robust innate laziness.

He drew a timeline and a spot on the timeline. The spot was one lie that I told. As the line progressed more dots climbed upward to represent all the lies that were required to cover the initial lie. Then he shaded the big curve created by the one lie and marked it *EFFORT*. Rob asked me to consider all the effort that was needed to protect one little lie.

And that is the true story of how I learned to be as honest as possible.

Thanks, Rob.

Obviously, I'm a natural emotional exhibitionist and that's not a great combination. The mail carrier does not care, in fact, how my day is really going.

Some people will behave as if they are scalded when you let the truth rip. You have to be careful and gentle with the truth.

You also have to be conscientious about sorting out what is actually the truth. If you start waving a bunch of half-digested items and claiming they are true, you'll wreck your credibility with your breakfast pals and might be asked to leave the most convenient McDonald's, permanently. You would deserve it, too.

There's often a difference between your truth and *the truth. The truth* can be proven. It's the stuff all reasonable witnesses will agree on, such as it is day time, the sun is shining, and my foot is on the ground, not on top of your foot and not on top of my head. If you want to say that my foot is ugly, that's not *the truth* as much as your opinion or your foot bias.

So, yeah, *the truth* mattered to me as a parent, and it still matters to me. I didn't pump my kids full of Santa Claus stories, precisely because I didn't think it was true. As a tiny weirdo, I remembered feeling very betrayed by the Santa hoodwinking.

My great-aunt disagreed. She was arguably the most sane individual I ever spent time with, and she still bought into the Santa mania. *It is magical* she insisted. It certainly didn't feel magical to me and may have been the existential crisis that led me to become such a dedicated lying kid.

What else have they wrought? As a tiny weirdo, I wondered.

It became very important to me, most important, in fact, that my kids feel they could trust me. I think they do, except for the smartest ones... who are all of them, or course!

My step kids had been punked completely with Santa lore and when one of them cornered me with her suspicions, I fessed up immediately. She was pissed off. I gently explained that parents think kids want to play pretend. She was stony, and feeling a taste of adult bitterness for the first time, she spit the story back to her younger siblings.

What a magical Christmas that was! In our imaginary family album, it is labeled as "The Christmas Mom Killed Santa."

Even though it was very uncomfortable and caused a storm of consternation, I've never regretted being honest with my newest kids. They know I would only lie if I had a very, very seriously important reason. They understand it must be a matter of lifesaving importance, not just that I'm cutting a corner for convenience.

When the necessity arises to lie in front of your kids, you need to consider what you are modeling. Be ready for a pointed de-brief from them.

We had one big family lie, while we smuggled a cat into a rental house. Having her was against the house rules, I had no time to find her a new home and on top of that, I didn't want to. I preferred to imagine that we were rescuing her from predatory hordes and saving her from extermination in the heartless urban ecosystem. The usual.

She was a lovely little cat who would one day elope with a wild cat pride, at least that's the way I like to imagine it. They made her queen of something despite her oversized rear legs and skittish tics.

I solemnly told the kids that we had to lie about Sally Cat. That was rule number one. Rule number two was that we had to only talk to each other about her and the difficultly of lying about her being in the house.

The baby couldn't even say "cat" yet, so that was easy. Getting the buy-in of the other kids was also very easy, alarmingly so. They would do anything to protect a small animal or a small person, if only so that they could torment it later.

I explained to the older kids that lying is taking the exit onto the highway of insanity, which is a terrible metaphor to use for a 10-year-old. Still, they understood what I meant. Poetry was driving them nuts at school.

So, we had a perfectly successful family lie and conserved that cat for her adventurous destiny of stubbornly hiding in a drainage ditch until she disappeared to begin her monarchy.

Bullshit

It's a waste of time hiding your true nature from your kids. They know who you really are and if they don't, they will figure it out. If my parents ever wanted me to provide an itemized list of all their foibles, I am ready. For some reason, they never asked me for that.

My stepfather liked to say that teenagers are like prison inmates. They have all the time in the world to scheme, steal and booby-trap the shed. In fact, I was never truly able to convince him that I was not a convict.

When he found some marijuana under my bed, nobody asked him why he was looking under my bed in the first place. I knew he looked because he was suspicious of that smell and just generally a suspicious person.

You can stand around with your crew cut and tell me how trustworthy you are, but if you snoop and assume people are tinkering with your possessions whenever your back is turned, I'm going to sort you into the shifty pile. In fact, he stole from his employers, and his basement was a museum of purloined office supplies. He wasn't a bad guy overall, but he was definitely a thief.

See how easy it is? We all know how to judge other people from the moment we can talk about someone who just left the room.

My stepfather has permanently left the room, so he won't mind a wee bit of honest character assassination, I bet.

His favorite expression was, "You can't bullshit a bullshitter." But, of course you can. It's America. If it's not America, well, then, it should be! You can bullshit anyone and on top of that you are entirely free to try. You can bluster about what a grown up you are and then have tantrums when anyone challenges your authority. It's your house and you have rights.

Your kids are not going to hold your illusions up for you forever, at least not if they are able to have their own little vision quest to reality. They will see your insecurity and delusion for the sad little personality turds they are.

Pretending to be someone else isn't for parenting, it's for the stage and screen. It's not your kid's job to be your fan, it's the other way around.

If you just happen to grow up to be someone worthy of admiration, that's pleasant for everyone. Well done!

Sanity

Refusing to grow up is refusing to really dig into your own mental health. Personal archeology is unpleasant and it certainly feels as if it can wait. Some people put it on hold until they die, right? Just like that weird neighbor who fills her house with garbage when she's not running a clown college, it's possible for you to keep so busy that you don't have to face the way you aren't facing your own damage.

It's fashionable to lament mild mental illness, and while that's certainly better than denial of disordered living, it's not the same thing as taking your mental health seriously. You have to work on it, beyond chasing happiness and tiny bubbles of feelgood-isms.

Nothing can distract you from developing your own mental health more strenuously than a baby. They are built for distraction and sleep deprivation. You need to get your emotional levers figured out before the kids get ahold of them. Otherwise, there is a danger that they will literally drive you crazy. That's where the phrase comes from, I'm pretty sure.

You need to determine what your problem is. Name it, identify its source, plan on how to solve it, move on to the next one because there is an endless supply of problems. If you have no problems, you are probably high, so it's only a matter of time before you trip over some problems you haven't noticed yet.

If you aren't clawing your way up out of boredom toward something you most value, you're going to soak in boredom until you don't even notice the cold any longer. Don't soak. Stroke! Swim for the hills, or something!

Some of us can get by with reading self-help books and having smart friends to talk to, but some of us are more like the me kind of us, who need a professional from time to time.

Therapy

How can you be sure your chosen professional is good for you? This is a terrible bind for the mad mommy. In our madness, we may not be able to assess who is truly helpful and who is inducting us into a cult.

Cults ask for money, but so do most therapists. Church folks, who arguably may be pulling you into their cult, sometimes do not ask for money.

Money is always a part of any difficult puzzle, but it's not your main concern here. You are worth the cost of the help you need. You are. No, you really are. Don't let the money stop you. You can work it out. A good therapist will help you figure it out.

Unfortunately, a bad therapist will help you figure out the money too. So how are you going to determine if the person you are working with is good for you?

They should provide a clear plan. Some people get involved in years and years of therapy without a goal. Feeling better is a goal, but what exactly does that mean to you? Better isn't a goal, but more of a journey. Your goal should be something like reaching a decision about marrying that clown, finding a job that doesn't make you cry yourself to sleep every night, making two new friends this month, or getting through a shopping trip without a panic attack.

People do all those things routinely, so why can't you? You can, but maybe you're stuck in a mental corner that seems like there is no way out. The proper professional can explain what's involved in turning you around and will have an estimate of how many sessions are needed before you begin to tiptoe out of the corner.

I have experienced everything from months of pointless complaining to nothing more than a prescription and a wave. Neither of these is the proper professional way. You're probably not a pro, so how will you know if you have a good fit, really?

In addition to having a plan, which you are included in, you should feel that you are loved by this person. It can be tough love, but you're smart, you know when you are loved. If they don't seem to be listening, they may not even notice when you say goodbye. It doesn't matter if he is your pastor and your dad's buddy, if you feel blamed and bullied, find someone else.

On top of providing an actual treatment plan and proceeding in a truly loving manner, they should give you homework and check it when you return.

Homework? What are you, twelve? Yes, just accept that in this problem you are twelve and you want to make thirteen, so do your homework. It's for you.

You can still get something out of mediocre therapy. Some of the best help I had was not great. The act of deciding to focus on the solutions and really thinking hard about where you are and where you're headed is important on its own.

Other people usually want to help, but they usually will not even attempt to help without an invitation. It's like the first rule of vampires without any vampires. If you resist asking for help, you might practice with small requests and build up from "Would you pass the ketchup?" to "Would you drive me to therapy?"

It will be okay, even when it's not okay yet.

You can count on you and if you can't, get busy on fixing that first.

Maturity

Even if you are not a fully mature parent, you will have your mature moments. Those are the times you help your kids identify their emotions with love and patience. At those magical times, you will be able to help them grapple with being a person in the world, feeling secure in their worth and strong enough to get out of bed and do good work, building a life they love.

Really? Really. It's not like that all the time for anyone, perfection is impossible. There will be days when you feel you can do little but whine, and then you'll sit on a cat and really regret everything. Even with the worst days, if you don't give up and remember all your efforts matter, you will have a lot of good days without need of perfection or unicorns.

Chapter 8
The Mistake of Assuming Kids Are Alike

Mild autism can give you a genius like Einstein. If you have severe autism, you could remain nonverbal. You don't want people to be on the severe end of the spectrum. But if you got rid of all the autism genetics, you wouldn't have science or art. All you would have is a bunch of social 'yak yaks.'
—Temple Grandin

People have studied genetics in the framework of modern science for a little while now. We have always studied genetics of people, long before the word *genetics* appeared. Those people used the armchair guesswork method, which is preferred by people who don't even have armchairs.

Genetics

You do not have to be certified in it to get genetics wrong. We all have the opportunity to screw it up.

For the purposes of family life, heredity is pretty much anything your family assumes it is. Sure, it's provably involved in things like being able to curl your tongue side to side. Go on and try it with a sibling now, I'll wait.

Proof aside, most families charge on willy-nilly to assume that they are born to be great at certain things and hopelessly talentless in other things.

Accepting limits of birth is a huge error. Listen for it when it happens and have a tantrum ready. "Our family is naturally terrible at math," or "All our kids are too clumsy for bicycles;" both of these doom the future of a cycling cipherer, at least a little bit. It's what we psychology armchair people call a self-fulfilling prophecy. Some kids are going to end up in the math circus. Why would you dissuade them from giving it a try?

What if your family is filled with criminals? Why are you reading this book? You should read something much more helpful before breeding a batch of little thieves.

By all means, pause and worry if there is some dreadful legacy looming and try to have a good understanding of what you can and cannot prevent. Even if you have to spend your Sundays at the prison because that's where all the aunties are right now, don't tell the kids it's their destiny. Let them figure that out. Maybe give them some extra tools to deal with their impulses.

Inheritance isn't the same thing as destiny. It may close many doors decisively, but there are always more doors to try. There is an exception to every rule, except for the rule that there's an exception to every rule.

Traits

The internal code may incline us this way or that, and knowing about it can give a kid a better boost. Arming them with understanding can help them lean the other way to compensate. After all, we want them to be balanced and effective and all that junk.

Caution is required. It's tricky to provide guidance without calling too much attention to their inclinations. There's a huge constructive difference between saying, "Dearest, you have no self-control," and "Dearest, I want to help you work on controlling more of your impulses."

There's no need to tell Dearest she's defective. Let her figure it out. Her defect belongs to her, after all, bless her pointy little noggin.

It's up to us to give them the tools they need to defend themselves, not the tools to hurt themselves. Telling a kid they are *stupid* or *lazy* or any of that isn't going to get you a prize winner in whatever you think is worthwhile, and if it does, they are going to be saying those same things to themselves all their pained lives. Life is painful enough, isn't it?

Point out the positives. Instead of calling her lazy, try: *You are so good at being horizontal! Let's try some vertical now! For science!*

This is hard to do if your own parents were heavy on the negative messages. It's well worth your trouble, however. The echoes of negativity carry on for generations.

When it's especially tough to stay helpful and it really doesn't feel like your child deserves your constructive spin right now, you can imagine you are doing it for your imaginary grandchildren instead. Think of little Belinda Joe basking in your support—now, isn't that nice?

We made a big deal of doing personality testing when the kids were mostly teens. This can be a terrible idea. It's fine if it is just a party game that gets everyone talking about what introversion means, but some kids will take that information far too much to heart. For me and a couple of the kids it was a long-term bummer: the foretelling of a CEO destiny can make one feel like a terrible slacker when one ends up parking cars.

And what about the kid who is somewhat introverted, who is told that they *are* an introvert. They are defined and then put a ton of energy into accepting a lie about their identity. A little gal may have a tendency to tunnel into private spaces to re-charge, but she is not on this earth to hide out all the time. We have to be careful telling little people who they are and focus more on who they are trying to become.

An introvert who wants to be more extroverted simply has a disadvantage in their starting point, just like the kid who wants to play piano but has only four fingers total. It's still doable. Kind of. Are you really going to be the creep who discourages that four-fingered child?

Mutants

Genetics don't determine who we can communicate with, or who we can love. We get to decide.

If we have disagreements with our kids or our neighbors or anyone, it's not about the genetics but the incomplete language and the broken assumptions of poor communication.

It's easy to blame traits, and who doesn't enjoy being lazy and operating from assumptions? We think we know something about short people or large eared types. Big hands mean generosity and big butts don't lie. Really?

It's best to remember that we're all on the same side in the fight against the real enemy: gravity.

Blanks

A baby doesn't appear as a blank slate, but they seem pretty close. They don't have language or culture or fear of chipmunks. They have so much to learn, it's easy to overlook their innate differences, but once you have spent time with two outwardly identical newborns, you see the peculiarities that are their little personality buds.

Some smile faster and others show astonishing grip strength. They can be passive or cranky, explorers or cuddlers, strippers or tumblers, anything is possible. Some babies are eerily adult, but that doesn't mean they're evil, they're just eerie. Maybe don't leave the knives out, just in case.

I was skeptical of people who said their babies had hungry cries distinct from tired cries and all the other cries. That was only because my first baby had a singular cry. Nobody knew what she was carrying on about, ever. "Dinner time!" sounded exactly like "Broken toe!" The only thing harder than trying to decipher a baby is being a baby.

I think it's a mistake to treat children, including babies, like empty vessels. It's tempting to think we can fill them up with our ideas and priorities and train them to cook us delicious food on holidays. We can try, of course. We all see plenty of evidence of that sort of effort around us. People are generally stubborn about getting their own way.

Babies and children are stubborn too, and I think it's because they are not empty at all. They are like little acorns that have all the instructions to become a particular type of tree Never mind that acorns make oaks: our tiny acorns can be any sort of giant in this example. It's not up to us to yell at them not to be a pine or a prickly pear.

Just because they have some tendencies of their own, that doesn't mean you want to encourage all their inclinations. A toddler who howls like a wolf is going to gain all the wrong kind of attention. I wouldn't throw them any meat during those episodes. Calmly remind them that if they want meat they need to ask politely, "Meat for me, please," with whatever capability they have at their stage. Don't assume they cannot understand or perform correctly, because one day they will, and that day might be today.

Babies

They progress through stages of development and can diverge at any point into different developmental hiccups. (If you want to read an expert, you can go back to Piaget. His book is much more elegant, and in French).

They appear to be very quick to learn a bunch of fears, but kids are never the same and their fears are not identical, either. If you pay attention, you will see that they are drawn toward different things and take notice of entirely different objects from an identical set up.

I took daily walks with Navy Bean and Garbanzo while I pushed Pinto Bean in a stroller. Navy Bean would halt the parade for a cool beetle, while Garbanzo was much more interested in the built objects the beetle might be crawling upon. Pinto Bean was most likely to sing a song to the beetle, or to eat it, depending on her mood. They were simultaneously having three different childhoods and it wasn't up to me at all.

It seems like a simple and obvious point, but parents screw this up every day. They try to wrestle a new kid into a previous kid's footsteps. Don't waste your time!

Because they are all different, you can't treat all the kids the same way. If your first kid is easy-going and portable, you may feel a burst of confidence so great that you are anxious to go ahead and make another kid. Classic mistake. The next kid will be immune to all your proven techniques, or at least most of them. He won't snuggle willingly into a car seat or accept any old blanket; he'll demand fealty and blood of an enemy before naptime. It's a whole new strategy set with a new kid.

Be as fair as possible and stick to your goals. You're getting the hang of this after two kids, after all. You know a few things about stuff. Maybe you should have a third kid. *HAHAHAHA*. Say goodbye to sanity.

Chapter 9
The Mistake of Worrying About Stages

When things go well for days on end,
it is an hilarious accident.
–Kurt Vonnegut

Of course, you should listen to experts, for instance, me! But you should also practice not listening to experts, because even the best expert is occasionally full of beans, also me! There are far too many self-appointed experts on parenting barging around telling people what they should and should not do with their kids.

Experts

If you get pregnant, you'll immediately sense this abundance of expert advice, assuming you speak the language of the people around you. Strangers on the bus will want to tell you their worst birth injury story, and random women in elevators will tell you about the time their water broke on that very elevator.

Take it all the way you take in weather forecast for a different continent. It's not your story they are telling, even as they very persuasively try to tell you it is. There might be some good information in there, sometimes it's helpful, sometimes it's just a story they love to tell anyone who will listen.

People get very worked up, defending their own decisions and projecting them all over other people, but that's no reason to go against your own best instincts.

On top of listing all the weird rashes kids can get, Dr. Spock's baby book advises very forcefully that parents pay attention to their own instincts and intuition in caring for their kids. Remember, your best instincts aren't going to be the laziest ones, but the loving and brave ones that may be just a little bit lazy.

Instinct may not alert you that changing crappy diapers immediately is important, until you see the connection between a sleepy pooper and a scary intergalactic yeast infection. But your instinct to comfort and hold an infant is exactly the thing to do, and anyone who tells you differently is probably selling snake oil and twirling their evil mustache while they do so.

Steps

Babies deserve the best of everything because babyhood is horrible. Most baby misery can be eased just by picking them up and holding them close. Can you believe that past experts have advised people not to hold babies too much? Can you believe that parents believed such a thing?

Some babies only get sweatier and crankier with holding, but the majority not only want to be held, but cuddled and rubbed and chatted up. The baby doesn't care if you can't sing on key, in fact, they are literally the least critical audience you will ever have for your nonsense, whatever it is. This doesn't hold up for toddlers, of course. As soon as my eldest could talk she started to hush me when I sang. "No Mama, don't sing," is a hell of a first sentence.

There are very few things you can do to screw up baby wrangling, which is good because you will be sleep deprived, at least for a few weeks. If you are in a modern arrangement, all you need to do at first is feed them, keep them warm, change their diapers promptly and properly, and get to the doctor at regular intervals.

A good doctor will alert you about problems to watch for, and I never did find a doctor who would directly tell me I was being neurotic about a baby's habits. They have heard nearly everything by the time they received a license.

Just because I assert that you shouldn't blindly follow expert advice, don't assume I mean you should bathe your baby in the moonlight and skip their shots. Do the science things. It's proven to keep tons and tons of babies alive. Don't mess with science unless you have much better science that works every time.

Skipping their immunizations can be tempting if you are fearful, but don't do the parenting out of fear thing, please.

One of my babies had a reaction to her first whooping cough vaccine. I hadn't read and retained the warning pamphlet that I signed, but it clearly stated that if the baby becomes unusually pale and limp, report the reaction. She may have gone quite pale, but the strange thing was the way she was so deeply unconscious after the shot that her little legs hung down to kick me in the knees. Normally, even sleeping, she kept her chubby little legs folded like a frog.

Her pertussis reaction was not subtle. Its description was right there in the hand out and once I re-read it, I called and talked to the pediatrician, even though the episode was over. While rare, her reaction was something they knew about because this immunization had been given millions of times. Her reaction wasn't predictable, but it was a known probability because of science.

She never had another pertussis shot because of that and she hasn't had whooping cough, at least not yet. While I can accept the good fortune this represents, it would be incredibly hard to accept the negative consequences if it had gone all wrong. She could have had a fatal allergic reaction or some other horrible outcome.

Sadly, someone's baby must be eaten by a dingo for the rest of us to understand and avoid the real dingo danger. We don't get a choice in the really dire consequences, and I'm sorry to have to keep pointing things like this out. It's just the way things work. Some babies are not going to make it to the next chapter of their lives and sometimes that baby is going to be our baby.

Once my daughter was old enough to anticipate the shots, we had to have a persuasive conversation in order to even get her through the doctor's door. I explained that shots might hurt for a second, but they would protect her from much more painful problems. She accepted this, but wanted to know if the shots would protect her from fire.

As much as I wanted to lie about that in order to reassure her, I said no, she would have to invent those shots when she grew up.

Babies, even in the very best health, are really relentless little jerks. I remember seeing two parents wandering the nighttime fairgrounds, looking more like zombies than any live people have a right to look. We noticed their distress too late, as we pushed our stroller baby opposite their stroller baby. Our stroller baby was snoring wetly and they looked at her with a weird, desperate gaze.

"Does she sleep at night, too?" they wanted to know. They hadn't slept for eight months, could not concentrate for any length of time, and the mom ended up running off to chase an imaginary monkey before the conversation was dropped with a thud.

My babies became better and better sleepers as I learned what worked. I am a huge fan of sleep.

It turns out, you do not have to be awake to breast feed, and sleeping in a comfortable chair is still sleeping. Because I didn't take any type of sedatives, I felt confident in sleeping with my babies close at hand.

However! Caution! Babies do suffocate, so you have to be mindful of keeping them out of beanbags and away from humans that might roll over on them in a stupor. Don't put them down on their stomach when they haven't learned any flippy tricks. Strong babies can sometimes un-wedge themselves from danger, but don't count on it because their inexperience and lack of reasoning is a huge disadvantage.

Enjoy them, even while you understand that they are total jerks. Remind yourself that this phase is short and precious, and they won't be entranced by the sound of your heartbeat for long.

Before you know it, they will be pressing, hard, on buttons you didn't even know you had.

Toddlers

You can give into young babies' whims without much worry, but once they are toddlers, you have to consider the consequences of your every surrender.

Don't hand them a stack of cookies or a stick of butter just because they demand it. You indulge such things at your peril. Ignore their bad behavior as much as possible and reward them only when they are in acceptable bounds for their ability.

You may think that all you want is one damned minute of peace and quiet. If you have to buy that one minute with a box of Quayzee Quackers, you shall have your minute of crunchy quiet, but it will cost you dearly in the longer run. That minute might matter a great deal, but usually it doesn't. If it's not that important, you have made a bad bargain and begun to pave a path to snack mania.

If you are on a call when you slip up in this way, you'll find that the phone becomes a source of snack attraction. When it rings, your little sharks begin to circle immediately with demands for Quackers or Jooose or NummyDumms. They knew that you became a vending machine before the idea ever dawned on you.

It's hard work to be thoughtful all the time you are awake. Children know this. They are not bad or sneaky in trying to get the better of you, well maybe some of them are bad or sneaky, but most of them are just trying to tinker with the way things work to get what they need and want.

If you aren't thoughtful about the way you reward and reinforce their little demands, you may help them begin to pave the way for confusing food with love or worse, confusing scolding with love.

Deviants

The way that any individual kid can be weird is unlimited. If I had a nickel for every time an experienced teacher told me they had never seen anything like one of my kids, I'd have a least a couple of nickels.

Just because they are non-standard in some way, that doesn't mean they are defective or that you are somehow doing parenting wrong. Some kids may be obsessed with small change or trying to get a peek at a penis, and some of their funkier pastimes may make you quite uncomfortable. It's your job to hide that discomfort and save the exorcist for the really serious stuff.

You can warn them that sneaking and peeking is likely to have the consequence of someone smacking them, but keep it matter of fact. Some kids have the goal of freaking you out for their amusement, so don't give them the satisfaction.

Ho hum, she's eating out of the sugar bowl again, no big deal. Perhaps calmly replace the sugar with salt and wait for the squeak.

Maybe she is stockpiling matches and seems to be planning something. Have her show you how to light the matches, but keep a pot of water handy in which she can stick her burned fingertips. Safer consequences are your allies.

These are not specific expert recommendations, of course, just things I did.

When you spy a young teen putting Irish Cream in her coffee, you can casually ask how long she has been going to school with whiskey breath. There's no requirement for you to tell everyone that she didn't know that real cream should be in the refrigerator. It's purely optional how much of a legend you create from it. It is all your fault, in any case.

Experts may tell you all sorts of unpleasant things with great conviction, but you should remember that you know your kid best. Why would you let a stranger give your kid a complex when you can do it yourself?

A stern old pediatrician told me that I was dooming my baby to a lifetime of obesity by letting her eat as much as she wanted when she was six months old. Seriously? It wasn't true then and it isn't true now. Fat babies have nutritional money in the bank and the added hilarity of being very easy to dress up like fireplugs for costume parties. Of course, you shouldn't feed your baby only dense calories, but a healthy baby cannot overdo it with healthy food that is actually food.

My babies that were the fattest and hungriest grew up to be the most indifferent about food. Had we been forcing them to eat, I suppose it would have ended up differently, but it was totally their idea to gobble everything in their way. Very rarely is a hungry baby clinically interesting, anyway.

The babies who won't eat cause all the worry. I didn't have any of those, but they happen, I hear. Some babies enjoy pacifiers, too, allegedly.

Pacifiers are considered dangerous by some folks, but their biggest danger in my observation is that they can get lost and precipitate a meltdown. Any kind of pacifier should be choke-proof and easily replaceable.

You'll learn. Practice babies are great for practice.

We had one avid thumb sucker in the bunch, and it was instantly obvious that the thumb was a kind of miracle of self-soothing. She wasn't going to lose her thumb, unless we had much bigger problems.

Her thumb fixation came abruptly to an end when she caught a cold and had to choose between sucking her thumb and breathing. With a tiny struggle she chose to breathe. Then she fixated on her navel, and it was imperative that she be able to stick her thumb in her navel at all times. Her overalls and onesies went into the donation pile. If she was dressed in a jumper that covered her belly button, she would claw at her clothes like a chimp in a bathing suit. Like so many scenes in parenting, it was equal parts upsetting and entertaining.

Experts suggested that a child with this level of oral fixation would become a smoker or a brass musician and you know what? Neither of those things came to pass. She eventually learned to soothe herself while keeping her clothes on and quit the trumpet in record time.

Stumping

Kids are always going to be weirder than you imagined and you will likely have an opportunity to stump the experts.

Listening to the experts is fine, in fact, it's never a bad idea to get another viewpoint. It can save you a lot of dithering around if you gain insight from whatever they say.

Don't let yourself be intimidated by their impressive titles if they have never had to improvise a barf bag in a swanky waiting room. You may not know what you're doing all the time, but you are doing it with love, right?

It's possible to paralyze yourself with reading about parenting. The choices and sources and findings only grow more boggling over time. One downside: it is possible to justify anything by finding some stray expert citation for that anything. As a person acquainted with people, you know that people can be passionately mistaken about anything. Anything goes, but does it?

If your strategy doesn't feel right or doesn't seem to be working, do a little research and ask around. An avid parent in your circle might have stumbled on something that will be a tremendous help. You'll only know about it if you ask.

Anybody who hasn't changed their views on children and parenting for twenty years is not a great source, and that includes dusty library books from the 1970s. Seventies parents were terrible: believe me, I had some. 1870s parents were even worse. They thought they were doing kids a favor by reminding them that they were likely to die any minute, every minute of the day. In fact, childhood was so grim back then it might cheer you up to read about it for perspective. Orphanages and jobs for little kids still exist, but at least now we can hope their norm is becoming a thing of the past.

Unfortunately, some parents will double down on their unsuccessful tactics. Don't be that parent. Don't be bonkers. If the way you are guiding your kids isn't working, try something else with love, for science!

Nutrition

Feeding kids without a side of drama is an important skill. It was not one I started out having, in fact I still struggle with it. Drama claims a place at the dinner table in surprising ways, even now.

Early on, I became obsessed with understanding how to apply the "food pyramid" to a baby diet. Parents today would chuckle at the way I stuffed my first baby full of carbohydrates, because they formed the base of that stupid pyramid. Those guidelines have been discarded now, and good riddance.

My intentions as a nascent nutritionist were the best, but it was impossible to perfect the baby's food system. Even if I portioned the vegetables correctly, how could one account for the portion that was spit back up? Did it count? I decided everything should count.

I mashed meat and vegetables into stupid shapes and tried to limit added sugar and salt. No peanuts were permitted and wheat had to wait. I was so good at feeding my little spud that the doctors were debating testing her for giantism before her first birthday. It's important to note: do not restrict fat for babies, they need fat for their fat little brains.

Are all my kids taller than I am because of fantastic feeding? Who cares!

Food is loaded with politics and confusion, just like that stupid pyramid. If you have restrictions of conscience, that is piled on top of the restrictions that you didn't even know you have. How did the chickens who laid your eggs get along? How far did that green bean travel? Who else died for your pork chop?

It's a lot to process before you even get to the processing.

I have some hard-won food beliefs, but they are mine and you don't have to be bothered about it unless you are coming over for Thanksgiving.

Currently, in our family we have more vegetarians than pescatarians, a smattering of carnivores, and there's always at least one person who is a lazy vegan.

I got to make the decisions about the food we had, because I did the shopping. If I didn't think it was healthy, I wouldn't buy it. My requirements for healthy food have become only more stringent. Local, organic and humane food products are a luxury, but if you had to pick only one luxury that's worth a big chunk of money, wouldn't that be the one? If you can grow your own whatever, why wouldn't you?

Junk

My mother *loved* to feed my kids junk food and it was a source of high tension. While they were little spuds, they did not know bread other than whole wheat existed. Gramma fixed that. She introduced free range soda and cookies into their lives and would cackle when I picked them up in the throes of sugar hangovers. Since her babysitting was free, she knew she had me boxed in and oddly flattened like a hostage HoHo.

My complaints were feeble, but bitter and pointless.

Some of my kids got the idea that food was more important than others did. Some of them will eat whatever gets in their path when they are hungry and others want to make sure their eggs are from happy chickens and no undue violence was employed in the manufacture of their vegetables.

Possibly because I took food very seriously—until I didn't and we got into the decade of pizza—they approach snacking with skepticism. Eating their feelings is still something they do, but hopefully with an awareness that it's happening by their choice rather than through some ravenous autopilot.

Preparing good food is an act of love, but it might not be the way you want to show your love when you have a large herd of children. Cooking is hard, and for some people cooking can be a soul-sucking adventure in failure as often as not. For some of us, the joy of cooking is only joyful if we have unlimited time, tons of practice and very loud music on.

Fortunately, you don't have to cook to feed well, as long as you have a bit of extra money for your food budget. It is possible to cheerfully live on salads and occasionally to get other people to cook for you; but the "cheerful" part will generally depend on how long it has been since you watched a documentary about factory farms or other food horrors.

With a pack of kids, opening a bag of carrot sticks is as easy as opening a bag of something loaded with additives and extra sugar. If you have good, clear food labels with nutrition information, and you can read them, you have no excuse for skipping that step. If you don't know what's in their food, what are you even doing feeding people?

You only have to learn a little bit about nutrition and shop like it matters. It also helps to shop like the center of the grocery store is radioactive, but in a fun way.

Aversions

For our family dinners, everyone was allowed to skip one food item at any time. Kids who hated shrimp didn't have to eat them. I might serve shrimp anyway if I forgot, and then someone could scramble an egg or microwave a burrito if there wasn't another solution on the table.

Everyone had to taste everything, as long as it wasn't their one hated item. In extreme circumstances, I might deem a dish skippable; for instance, if the chicken was somewhat raw. I would not insist they join me in Salmonella Land. I'm not a total monster.

My reasoning for all this was simple enough; no one had forced me to eat, in fact, there had been times when

I was very hungry as a child, and nobody was bothered about that either. I learned about food independently, by trial and error. Eventually, I did not eat handfuls of chewable vitamins, and I probably didn't eat too many paint chips. I was indifferent to food. It was something that happened at intervals and was almost never anything to get excited about.

I was never like that uncle who began to breathe heavily around a ham, and I guess I never will be. It wasn't a great way to be, but it meant that I was a fairly blank slate when it came time to learn how to prepare food for myself and other people.

For me, mashed potatoes were not love, although butter was close.

Since most people talk far too much about food and their feelings surrounding food, if you have been paying any attention to anything, you know how quickly things get weird.

Some people feign food allergies when they actually have a standard issue aversion to something like asparagus. You are allowed to hate asparagus. Anyone who argues about that has trouble with the part of their brain that reminds them to shut up and let people skip what they want to skip.

If you have a little kid that refuses to eat anything except hotdogs and peas, there are at least three problems with this. Hotdogs and peas do not form a balanced diet, and it doesn't matter if she is making serious money in her video career, you are the adult and you need to put some other stuff on the plate. Third is the matter of even allowing hotdogs around small kids. Are you a bit too excited about giving Heimlich's? It doesn't matter how organic the dogs are if you choke on them.

Don't surrender the dietary choices to the tots. Sure, she may claim that she will hold her breath until Santa comes to bring her a new family. It's your job to let her try and not laugh too much at her when at last, she doesn't get her way.

Awareness of serious food allergies was just beginning to surge around here when my kids hit school. It's very important to be respectful of people's dietary problems. Usually they are caused by something far outside their control, like George Washington Carver's historic peanut mania. Maybe people shouldn't eat so many peanuts and maybe bread isn't the daily bread of every daily person. What do you care? Let them skip what they need to skip and trust them to be quiet while you eat your dolphin sandwich. The important thing is that we're all alive to eat whatever, for the time being.

Chapter 10
The Mistake of Narcissistic Expression

Having a baby dragged me, kicking and screaming,
from the world of self-absorption.
— Paul Reiser

Narcissism draws a lot of criticism and loathing as a trait, but it's an unfair burden. In its most benign form, narcissism is self-regard, typified by lovingly staring at one's own reflection in a calm pool of water. What really needs to be vilified is the hardened destructive narcissism that grows from those harmless beginnings of baby ego. Don't be confused: a little vanity is like a tiny acorn in comparison to the rampaging oak tree of unchecked ego.

Narcissism

Babies are narcissists, and correctly so. It's one of the few things they have going for them. They need to be cute and gravitationally attractive to other humans if they are going to survive. They cannot appreciate how adorable they are, but that is just because they are so mired in their own cuteness and it is all they are aware of.

Children and teens are also narcissists by nature and there's little point in berating them for it. They'll have plenty of chances to slap up against the reality of other people's viewpoints. They will generally grow out of narcissism, just like their terrible shoe choices.

I suggest that in the meantime, we gently point out other people's feelings and priorities in an instructive way. "Now, Bean, do you understand why your sister thinks your chewed food is disgusting to look at? Would you want to see her lunch more than once?"

The tipping point for the narcissist comes when they begin to believe deep down that no one else has a deep-down life. Other people are less real in this set up and can be viewed as tools or cogs in the only "real" machine that is the narcissist's life.

Narcissism changes from a survival stage to a disorder with time and practice. Some people learn it from masterful demonstration by a parent—or holy cow—sometimes both parents. When your individual personhood is relentlessly overlooked for long enough, it begins to seem like the natural way of things. It is your job to admire, fear, and obey the will of your masterful demonstrator.

You may begin to believe you don't matter; in which case you will have found the saddest pathway of escape from narcissism. In this scenario, you sideline yourself and cast yourself in a supporting role.

At least you can feel good about not being a tyrant, waving the banner of your own self-importance as you instead tiptoe carefully into your own little life. With any luck you may develop a healthy sense of yourself after all, but don't expect any help from your bullies.

For those who discover the power to wield the knife of narcissism on others, essentially everything that can go wrong with relationships will go wrong. Barging all over other people's feelings and demanding that they appreciate *What You Are Going Through* is only the beginning of doing it all wrong.

Raising children as a narcissist is entirely possible and entirely inadvisable. Try to park those tendencies like your life depends on it, because it's that important. If you can't respect your children's feelings and separate identities, you will not only miss the most delightful part of parenting, you will risk scrambling their little hearts and perpetuating a disease that steals joy from everyone in its reach.

That may sound like an exaggeration, and if I had a nickel for every time I've been accused of exaggerating, I'd have all the nickels in Wisconsin, but it's not wrong in spirit. Narcissism is parental poison. People spend their entire lives trying to untangle the effects and still live uncomfortably in the suburbs of Me-ville.

It's not the only bad thing, but it is very, very bad.

So, when you're wrestling with recovery from a childhood that starred a narcissist, you should do the exact opposite of whatever they would do, right?

That's a trap. Don't fall for it. Whatever your parents' damage, doing exactly what they did or exactly the opposite of what they did is not the answer. You have to engage your noggin and work it out on your own. Expressing a super free-range philosophy because you were cooped up as a kid may or may not be the best choice. If you live in a dangerous location, letting your kids play in traffic isn't freeing them, it's more like inflicting them on innocent commuters.

Hey, it's good you are thinking it over, whatever you are thinking. You don't want to reflexively copy or be a reflexive anti-copycat for whatever went on during your childhood. Reason with yourself. Spend a good long time thinking about and deciding on the sort of parent you want to be.

Now if you are narcissistic about it, you'll work out how you want to be *perceived* as a parent. Maybe you want to appear to be just and wise. Maybe you want to be beloved and revered. This is also a trap. Don't fall for it.

It makes no difference how you wish to be perceived. It's like wishing to be two inches taller, which accomplishes less than nothing. What matters is the parent you will actually become.

I always wanted to be the serene and endlessly patient parent that I imagined my Grammy was. This was the set up for some pretty standard disappointments. For one thing, my ideal was not a real person, but rather a caricature—an image based on a real person with comically oversized patience. This person, who I had witnessed losing her marbles on more than one occasion, was not perfect, but she did put a great deal of effort into maintaining a bubble of serenity around herself. She made me feel safe, and I hoped to make a bubble for my little bubs in the same way.

It felt horrible when I failed to keep this up. When I could not maintain my calm demeanor, the distress I was feeling was made much, much worse by feeling that I was *failing as a mother* on top of whatever my anguish was. I went to some lengths to hide any of my conniptions from my kids. Among those lengths was yammering endless complaints to anyone who would sit still, writing bizarre poetry and then setting it on fire, and daydreaming about catastrophes until I gave myself an ulcer. Some hobbies truly are better than others.

It might have been easier to have the goal of being a *mostly* calm and benevolent mom. You can cut yourself some slack, the way you can with extremely casual housekeeping.

My beloved grandmother was an excellent housekeeper and a big ole narcissist; so I must conclude, with the gift of a pretty interesting menu of emulations, it's probably best to go a la carte.

Reflections

Your kids are also not a reflection of you, even though sometimes other people may say so. You would not buy the criticism if your kid was a notorious gangster, would you? "Hey, I gave him toaster tarts, but I didn't encourage him to build a crime empire out of tarts or anything."

If you're not to blame for the outcome, you can't claim credit for it either. They make their own choices and no matter how hard you try to steer them, they still hold the wheel—or the rudder or the bong.

When I didn't land in jail by twenty-two, there were relatives lining up to pat each other on the back for the way I reached maturity without being an obvious criminal or community nuisance. Baloney! I could have turned directly to crime at any moment and made them all pipe down. Heck, I still might.

Many of us have the tendency to judge others by the outcomes their children display, but do we even know how the children really live? Everything may look just fine and be internal damnation. The kids may be in a rough patch of hooliganism that will benefit their future well-being tremendously. Who's to say?

You would be much better off judging people by how clean their dogs are or how their house smells or how often they nag you for money. No matter what your method, you can never be certain if you are judging people correctly, so maybe knock it off and wash your own dog.

Naming

Kids deserve the chance to be their own people. I don't recommend naming them for anyone else. People do this all the time, after all, there are only so many names, right? Why not name your daughter Catherine The Great Smith? Maybe because it's a burden, like naming her Judge Catherine Smith. What if later she has uncertain ambitions? What if your spouse has a best friend named Catherine who then becomes her sworn enemy? Baby Judge Catherine is going to be in even more trouble. Just don't.

Naming is hard, so let's take it seriously. You can junior around if you want to, most people will shrug it off, it'll be okay, but maybe give Benjamin Franklin XV a break and let him have his own name instead of recycling yours.

Vicarious

Many parents don't even notice how thoroughly they are living through their kids. If you are taking all their situations personally, wrapped up in your own replay, you are missing their play.

It's harder to push them if you step back now and then. Sure, you thoroughly enjoyed karate, but it might not be the best hobby for Little Lima Bean. She might have tender feet that just can't take all the kicking and stubborn fungus. Maybe she'd rather keep her shoes on and play chess.

But it will build character, you think. Fine, so will chess. She's only eight. Let her take a few years to warm up to the idea of kicking strangers, why don't you? If you are pushing Little Lima Bean into a stinky gee anyway, what is really on your mind?

It's hard for anybody to keep the balance, but it's even harder if you have a narcissistic base of operations. Maybe your own training was mainly in how to give up on every possible pastime, to the point that your gold medal in quitting sits gathering dust on your mantle. Do you want to hand down that legacy? Are you giving your son a hard time for sticking with clarinet because you never did stay with it, or because he still sounds terrible after two years? It matters. Earplugs exist, you know.

Some kids will stick with activities they don't really enjoy simply to please the parents. How many movies about that have we been forced to watch? Doesn't your heart go out—right through your throat—to watch a little gal as she climbs the ladder to do the tightrope walk against her wishes, driven by extreme people-pleasing as she directs them to remove the net. *This can't be good*, you predict. You are so smart!

The choice comes down too often to push or not to push. Ideally, kids choose their own suitable passions and have a chance to pursue them without a lot of fuss or illegal equipment.

If they have something that involves exercise, fresh air and collaboration, I think you can safely forgo the pushing. If they also want to hole up with games for an afternoon, you can allow it with a clear conscience as long as some dank and lonely pastime isn't their only hobby.

Hobbies

I pushed some kids here or there, but the quitting was most definitely my main struggle. They quit plenty of things; gymnastics, karate, ballet, lacrosse, flute, tap dancing, violin, track, acting, trumpet, cheerleading, guitar, football, and others I don't remember because they didn't require equipment.

Nobody in our crew quit everything, eventually they each found a group or hobby that really suited them, and somehow unlike me their groups weren't a bunch of drapes[12] whose chief hobby was smoking cigarettes and avoiding work. Amazing!

---

[12] *Drapes* is a term possibly coined by John Waters to describe *greasers* in 1950s Baltimore. *Greasers* also appear in the film "Grease" and were roughly correspondent to *freaks* in my generation. Kids today have the good sense to use the word *people* for such people, I hear.

Graduations

After each graduation, I was afflicted with a terrible ache. Not that I was sorry to see the end of the phase for the kid; rather the ache was all mine. As a young one, I had wasted my own time so stubbornly and quit so emphatically that I had quit myself out of nearly every opportunity.

We can't prevent our kids from having their own regrets, but we can most definitely prevent our kids from having to deal with our regrets.

Looking back stings, but you don't have to dwell there and you don't have to take a tour of the past with your kids. Imagine what a revolting expedition you could craft of all the sites where you had your greatest disappointments. "Here's the spot where the pothole destroyed my first skateboard, and here is where I called a classmate names to try to fit in... and over there is the basement where I saw my first angry penis."

Let's not look back. Let's just make some new mistakes instead.

Failures

Some kids are more risk shy than others, but none of them start out genuinely enjoying failures. What is more painful than putting in your full effort and working with maximum intensity only to be passed over or made some kind of understudy? Shingles. Shingles is more painful, but that's beside the point.

Once your kid has been smacked down by a failure or a second-string result that they consider a failure, watch for their next step. They may retreat completely from the field and with rare exceptions, this is a mistake, a greater failure, if you will. Even worse, some parents will hand them a big old platter of sour grapes and point out all the reasons they didn't want to be on that stupid team or in that stupid first flute chair.

Maybe the team or the chair is actually stupid and maybe the game is rigged, but the important thing is helping your kid navigate their desire and disappointment. Did they miss something they could do better next time? Are they absolutely sure they want to work that hard again to try for first place? Did they get some satisfaction from the effort itself? What have you learned, Dorothy?

Fall down six times and get up eight times, or something, right?

The thing that is easy for kids to miss is that failure and other surprising outcomes can be positive experiences. Sure, the sting of rejection is painful, but none of us can experience acceptance without rejection tagging along or riding shotgun. Hiding out from failure and rejection is never going to make us healthy and happy, it will just make us good at hiding.

A few of my kids, quite to my surprise, became invested in Certamen during high school. It's essentially a Latin quiz competition where someone pretends to argue with Homer about classical facts, or something like that. I never attended any of the events, so it's not clear what really happened, but they cheerfully reported on their failures each time. Third place of three teams was the usual result, but they kept at it because they adored the teacher and the spirit of the exercise, and they probably were gaining some extra credit too.

When they finally won a second-place ribbon, you would have thought that Michael Phelps[13] had just swum through our living room. It was a big day.

I think the keys are helping the kids take their struggles not too personally and pride themselves on the effort itself. That's not to say that giving everyone participation medals[14] is the answer. Rather, being second is okay and not being included at all is okay too. If a kid isn't the best at a thing, they simply have not found their thing yet. Everybody has a thing.

Just because a gal is a second-chair trumpet, that doesn't make her a second-chair human or you a second-chair parent. Why not be happy there are plenty of chairs, instead?

Letting them fail is going to be hard for your narcissist, but let's all give our inner narcissist as much trouble as possible. Don't let it drive the family crazy for the sake of its image.

---

[13] Michael Phelps was a local legend, who was also a world-famous swimming person, who had, not incidentally, outrageously long arms. He probably still has them.

[14] Providing participation medals was a move made popular in my youth. Some people still carp about it as if the medals are making kids soft or needy, but really it's just a good strategy for little kids and a questionable strategy for those who can reason and learn how to not win all the time, accept reality for the mixed bag it is, and so on. You know, grown-up stuff.

Chapter 11
The Mistake of Assuming You Understand Supervision

*Mom would pack our lunch and send us off with
no supervision. There were enough of us
so that if she lost a few, there
would still be plenty left.*
—Jeff Lowe, Alpinist

Before we go on to cover supervision of kids, you need to understand that parents need supervision even more; not official supervision, although if you're a dope about it, you may encounter that.

Supervision

In my state in the 1990s, you had to endure more screening and scrutiny to adopt a stray animal than you did to take a baby home from the hospital.

By the close of the decade, the Catholic hospital where most area babies were joining the party had ramped up its education sessions. I was furious that they would delay me with diapering lessons. After all, I had been changing diapers for a solid six years by that time, and could quite literally make any diaper work on any flailing tiny butt, upside down and in my sleep. It's only now that I hope I didn't hurt the social worker's feelings too much when I bolted. Like a true gangster, I pried myself out of my plastic chair and waddled away to do more diapering and parenthood.

First-timers accept that they need some instructions, and I suppose that it's good to have some trained people giving instructions instead of blindly accepting the suggestion from an elderly uncle urging you to you slip some booze in a glass milk bottle for your little nipper. That is a terrible idea. Don't dabble in baby poison. Just because it used to be common doesn't make it even adjacent to a good idea.

The fashions of feeding aside, there are plenty of baby facts that do not change. I read everything I could and consulted as many different people as possible. While that is the hardest way to spare confusion, it creates a nice, wide base to decide which things to ignore.

One of my aunts watched me with my first baby and declared that I was too quiet. I was actually a quiet person, in a mildly sinister way. She chided that the baby would never learn to talk, having a grim, efficient mom swabbing and swaddling her. Babies need to be spoken to in order to get the idea what talking is for. *Narrate constantly*, was her advice.

That wasn't in any of my baby books, but it felt entirely correct, so I followed her advice: no baby talk, but constant chatter and nattering. Little Navy Bean spoke more than a dozen different words by her first birthday.

Total strangers will judge you and try to tell you what to do with your kids. It's annoying, it's intrusive and it is part of being in a society. Your kids are the future for them too. If your kids develop into jerks with germs, it matters to the larger community, and if you aren't in a larger community, you may be doing parenthood the very hardest and most perilous way. Maybe get off the mountain more.

So, proceed with confidence, just not total confidence, and question yourself regularly, "Am I doing my best here? Is this the right message? Should she go to school in her pajamas for one more day?"

Minimalists

When my brother was a toddler, his mom and our dad would turn him loose in the shopping mall. I was horrified by this and would follow him obsessively while they sat sipping coffee and laughing at me.

It was a few years before I learned to relax about all that. After all the time I spent chasing him around and paging him when he outran me, I finally understood it wasn't all my job. If I didn't chase him, he wouldn't run.

When my brother was with me in a store, bored while I searched for the perfect party dress, he got stuck behind a rack of clothes where he couldn't see me. He screamed for me, "I'm lost!"

Who doesn't love a good collaboration? We could both worry about where he was from that point on, and I never worried as much about his whereabouts again.

Stranger danger was widely ignored when I was a kid, and back then most parents still thought child predators were as unusual as marauding lions. It was something my mother chose to worry about, and because of paranoid parenting, I was confined a lot, sometimes for months at a time.

While my friends were at horse camp, I was marooned in the basement of Camp Grandparents, studying the paneling and wondering how my entire body could itch at the same time.

It was a miserable way to spend summers; all to avoid a little crime. So, with my own kids, even understanding that the lightning bolt of crazy kidnappers is an actual hazard, I decided it was better not to pump my kids full of the fears I had been fed as a little gal.

I had been forbidden from walking home from school through a small wooded park "because of kidnappers." By the time I was about eight years old, I reasoned that kidnappers wouldn't want me, because we were poor and I'd learned from television that kidnappers only wanted money. So, despite the forbidden zone, I started cutting through the woods after school. Nothing bad ever happened, but there was this glowing sense of danger and rebellion that would go on to inform my terrible teens.

I didn't want to reproduce that particular set of events with my reproductions, either.

Their situation was significantly different and more dangerous, due to the absence of daytime neighborhood adults. When I was a kid, we swarmed into each other's homes, rooted out the snacks, and then heaped in front of a tiny television or rummaged through games as a pack to find one game to scuff a little more. Some mom or other always knew where we were.

As the latch-key kid business began to boom, the mom patrol wasn't nearly as formidable. Kids were warned more and more and kept safe with a new neighborhood alienation. By the time I was a teen, every excursion was like a jailbreak and every neighborhood felt haunted in the daylight.

When I took my first toddler to the playground, I was deeply distressed that other little kids shied away from any conversation with me. Kids used to love me, I bet.

These new kids avoided talking to me even in their own homes. As I came to learn, their moms had drilled them so thoroughly on Stanger Danger they wouldn't talk to anyone. The way I had been hemmed in and drilled with warnings had become the favorite method of moms everywhere we went.

I didn't like it, so we had a different approach to strangers. I told my kids they were welcome to talk to strangers, but they should always remember that some strangers are up to no good. For that we had two rules: stay well out of grabbing distance and don't believe they need your help. They have candy or a puppy? Nope. They ask you to help them find something? Nope. Those are both hallmarks of a bad stranger.

Logically, we know that the real dangers to kids are the most familiar people. They are also endangered by the most familiar things, like automobiles, and guns, along with hotdogs, peanut butter, buckets of water, buckets of balloons, things they can get trapped inside and anything that can form a noose.

Being born is also a very dangerous way to meet a stranger.

I thought my responsibility was to make safe spaces for my kids to explore: cleaning just often enough that they didn't get their knees too grubby while crawling around the house, for instance. Chemicals were stored in the highest cabinets and latched. If there was a table with a deadly corner it needed to be stored in the kid-free zone until they learned not to trip and fall on it—in other words, forever.

It's hard work to supervise this way, and it still doesn't prevent accidents. Accidents are the things you didn't think of: the baby who has never rolled before, then rolls off a bed to thump on the floor, or the kid who never showed any interest in such things suddenly decides to fly.

Never forget that they are constantly trying to get killed. The sooner you accept that you need to conserve your energy and try *just enough* to prevent serious injury, the happier everyone will be.

I patrolled for fire ant nests frequently and routinely and still had some get into the crib and bite the baby. Nightmares and instant phobia for all!

Even as I was obsessed with safety, I still had to call poison control and I still took kids in for stitches and casts, because the rest of the world is not obsessed with making kids safe. Nor should they be! Some kids will need to find out for themselves that gravity is a law they cannot ignore.

I also took up the responsibility to supervise other kids in the neighborhood and not only because they sometimes appeared in my home. When one of the gals was pushed by a big kid at the playground, I gave the pusher a stern lecture about never shoving little girls, even if they were being total maniac banshees.

His version of events was entirely plausible and entirely irrelevant to the lesson. Whatever else happened, that child did not grow up without pointed instructions on bullying smaller children. I never had to call his parents about any incidents, either.

One sober mom per block isn't enough, but it's better than nothing.

The early years are brutal, but if you can withstand it, by the time everyone is in grade school and middle school, you will only have to ask a few questions and hand out bandages and popsicles, like a 1970s parent.

I made them roam, but in groups. The buddy system is an actual system not to be sneezed at. It works. Three kids are probably not optimum, however, because one of them is usually singled out and may be picked off by passing hyenas.

It's not the 1940s any longer. The days of putting five-year-olds on public transportation are probably gone, but twelve-year-olds should be hopping on a bus to go see a museum in town, depending on the town and the kids, of course. Under the right conditions, they will see too much of humanity and they will be better prepared and better humans for it.

Assuming you are trying to get them ready to be Out There, they need skills. If they are going to thrive, life skills need to come from life, not just reading and watching other lives. They can't learn how to do things with their hands only by reading, they have to get their hands dirty and try to do things with other people.

Otherwise, they are self-taught to play guitar upside down and have to spend a bunch of time convincing everyone it was on purpose.

They should have stories to tell you so you can help them understand the experiences they are having. Telling you the plot to the latest cartoon they consumed is fine but it's not the same thing.

Your job is to get yourself fired from supervision. If they make decisions about who to trust and how to deal with gravity, they will get better at reasoning such things.

I suggest you stay uncomfortable with their limits so that they can keep pushing them out further, particularly the teens. They love to make you squirm, so let them. Giving them greater privacy will help, but they will still find ways to sandpaper your nerves. It's natural! If you really hate the tattoo, never let them suspect. If you show your dislike, you are just begging for more bad tattoos.

Giving oppositional teens some beneficial things to rebel against is a great strategy. Discourage them from brainy clubs at school and watch them become the President of Latin Quizzes. Give them the choice between odious after school chores or an after-school job and see those paychecks stack up.

Independence

If they lean on you too much, don't fall for the comfort of regression. It's a trap, like a lazy lounge chair. Instead, you want them to be independent so they can start having lives you can envy. If they start backing up and shrinking their worlds, nudge them forward with your intermittent full support, like the first time riding a bike.

Do you want to find yourself dropping a kid off at college and worrying about their ability to find decent food? Of course not. Will Soybean be able to find a burrito and wrangle with a rowdy roommate? Will Mung Bean spend a full day crying in a library bathroom or will she teach every kid on her floor how to fold their underwear? Both?

I've seen parents who grill their kids on prime numbers and that's cute, but it's not going to help if that son can't calculate how many beers he drank from that funnel. Don't neglect the basics.

Technology

It's tempting to rely on technology, but ordinarily you do not have to use baby monitors and nanny cams and dash cams. Your personal attention is more work and much more valuable.

We set up a spy camera during one vacation and spent far too much time monitoring Soybean's illegal science kid party. *Was that a beer?* We peered at the grainy image from 500 miles away. *Is whassisname sleeping in my chair?* We were so creepy, and nothing was learned except that we were so creepy.

If you think your teen is going to throw a Risky Business soiree, maybe hire the most trustworthy neighborhood sex workers to housesit instead.

Without an actual felony to witness, the nanny cam you bought is only doing good for the nanny cam company.

Eggshells

Perhaps some country schools still hatch chickens in second grade. We did, and while I was supposed to learn the phases of development, I learned something else entirely. When I raised some chickens with some of my own kids many years later, I taught them the same thing: the chick has to get out on its own, so don't help it.

I broke that rule and helped a struggling chick escape its shell. She couldn't stand up or get close enough to the hen to stay warm, so I kept her in my bra for the rest of the day—the chick, not the hen. I talked to her and encouraged her to stand up, but she died instead. I knew it was hopeless, but I hoped I was wrong. Such, sometimes, is hope.

Don't be like me.

The chicks have to escape on their own because of bird logic that can't be denied. If they can't get out of the shell on their own, they should not get out at all. It's their first solo battle.

Now children are not birds, usually, but we can't be entirely sure where and when their solo battle will pop up. If we are constantly paving their way, they are missing chances to see what they can do. It's annoying, watching a toddler drag a chair that you know full well is not going to help them reach the top shelf, but sometimes the best thing you can do is give them a minute to fail.

Some parents embrace this concept too heartily and create failure scenarios by throwing their kid in the deep end of the pool. Sometimes it's an actual pool, too. That's a bad idea, even if you are a lifeguard.

Life has a way of presenting those deep ends and obstacles, and you don't have to manufacture the situations, especially if you are a bit too casual about supervision.

One of my lowest moments came from a lapse of supervision with one of my wiliest children. Some kids need more surveillance, because they are more likely to try to invent rockets and such. You may already know which kid, but their inventive impulse may burst on the scene without warning. Any kid can be that kid.

Of course, I had ample warning in this case, but I was occupied with paying work or some other triviality when the phone call came. Two of my children had appeared at the neighbor's house, naked except for *mardi gras* beads.

Even in the scope of "Lord of the Butterflies" incidents, this was noteworthy. The kids had decided to visit the neighbor, and had deduced that they could follow the creek to get there. They had traveled about a mile by water. The nudity wasn't explained; they probably decided it was best for swimming.

One gal was very keen to tell me that she had carried the baby through the rapids. Now, because it was a creek, I knew there was no actual white-water zone. The idea that the water was deep enough that she had to swim while clutching a toddler, and had the temerity to be proud of herself as if she were some pioneer child fording a river to get anti-venom, well, no, that was not acceptable. There's bored and then there's chaos engine bored.

Our pioneer had to be deflated and made to understand that she did not have license to float the baby anywhere without express permission, the world is not her bathtub, and she probably broke a couple of laws. She was embarrassed so deeply that further punishment was not necessary. More punishment certainly happened, anyway. She never did that again, but went on to invent other near-calamities of lesser seriousness and greater clean-up.

My horror and embarrassment could not be overstated, but I was getting used to it by then.

Docile

Because of the way inertia works, or doesn't work, it's easy to neglect the really easy kids. Supervision of the kids who don't seem to need it is every bit as important as supervising the kids on the verge of berserk.

A kid who stays out of focus, gets grades good enough to slide through school without making waves is a kid who could use a little more positive attention. Notice how they spend their time and who captures their interest. If they are super helpful and eager to please, they could be covering some behaviors that they are sure would displease you, like systematically de-flowering all the neighborhood boys. Everybody needs a hobby, but it's better to know what it is so you can nudge them back on track toward more worthy goals.

The super helpful kid will also be the one who, if they trust you, will tell you there's a flotilla of toddlers heading downstream. They know things.

Crashing

Some kids will crash and I'm sorry. You may have to drive to a hospital wondering if they will recover. It's awful and it's part of the job as much as poop and pain. You can't spell *renting pain* without *in parenting.* Or something.

So, yes, I have had a few horrible phone calls that turned out to be something mostly tolerable, like a car repair. The kids are now trained to start all such conversations with, "I'm fine, but..."

I hope that no one reading this ever gets a call from a neighbor they don't know to tell them that their kid is being cut out of a car. We got that call, but only once so far.

She was home from college on Mother's Day, and I remember clearly being worried in that random maternal way about her packing her bicycle in the back of her car to ride alone in the country. Maybe I was only worried in honor of Mother's Day, but she was so beautifully fragile. She was determined to "get buff" over the summer to fill out her spindly teen limbs. I wanted that for her too, so she could punch anybody who tried to hurt her.

She never had a chance to punch the driver who hit her. I had the chance, but I didn't punch them, probably because there were too many witnesses.

Despite an uneventful bike ride, my little gal crossed paths with a reckless driver. The other driver was distracted by the presence of some fries and a free cat in their car. There was video of the prelude to the crash, in which the vehicle crossed the center line many times until the last time when it was stopped by colliding with my kid's car.

May you never turn a corner to see the wall of strobes of every emergency vehicle in town. The panicky surge of emotion is so overwhelming that it retracts somewhere, somewhere out of sight and useless at such a time, possibly into your sinuses.

You wish the ambulance driver a happy Mother's Day, even though you are having the most unhappy one you ever heard of. You are able to answer all the important questions because your kid has the most boring medical profile of all time; no allergies, no surgeries, she's just chronically sarcastic, like Deadpool.

She tells you she woke up with glass in her mouth and you still don't punch anyone. Detachment, it turns out, is a miracle bestowed on fans of fries and free cats.

Anyway, she loses the summer of *buffness* to a summer of recovery filled with casts and walkers and such. The reckless driver is charged and skips town to destroy someone else's car another day. No one can be sure, but I am convinced the cat skipped town too. Maybe its shot at freedom was the reason the accident had to happen. We can't know.

Your kid's innocence is sticking out like a big, silly chin.

You can't supervise enough to prevent disaster, but definitely teach them how to be chronically sarcastic, just in case they need it.

Chapter 12
The Mistake of Assuming You Understand Discipline

Instant gratification takes too long.
–Carrie Fisher

Good parenting doesn't feel good. Your mom probably tried to tell you this for a long time. Sure, there are moments of satisfaction, but the key here is the word "moments." Telling your kids, "Someday you'll thank me," does not guarantee that they will ever remember to thank you, but it's a neatly passive aggressive way to remind yourself there's a payoff in there somewhere, maybe.

Discipline

Indulging kids is a great joy, but it's not your joy, good parent. Leave it to Grandma to let them gnaw a tunnel through Cookie Dough Mountain.

Your mission is much more difficult. If you surrender the notion of being pals at the beginning, you can't be disappointed. Think this one through: did you ever really want to be pals with your parents? Did you want them to confide in you like a friend? Are you sure?

Ask anyone about the times their parents crossed that line. That line is generally a scar. No, your kids don't want to know about your misadventures in sex. No, do not elaborate on the time you were plowed in a car.

Time will wear down any mystique you throw together, but I strongly suggest you wear a parent suit under your parent suit. That is discipline and it is uncomfortable.

Control

You are obligated to control your kids. They might disagree with this, but they appreciate your efforts to keep them contained and safe from their own worst impulses. They will work hard to get around you, but they notice that you care when you hide the candy or toss up other obstacles to their excesses.

"Why do you keep buying the crappy orange juice?"

"Because you'll only guzzle the good stuff."

Keeping them controlled is a tiny fraction of discipline, but it seems to be the one that new parents have the most curiosity about. They think that their own hyper vigilance is the key, but it's not. What you *do* most consistently speaks the loudest in this power struggle.

At a critical point in my skirmish with energetic toddlers, a friend suggested I be ready always to escape and quit an expedition. The idea that I could pull an invisible rip cord and drop right out of the hardware store at any point was a revelation. Whenever the baby screeched, I would start a countdown to cancelation of the situation. I loved disappearing when it got weird. It was my favorite mommy magic trick.

While it was freeing, we can take it too far. I did not consistently power through rowdy story times or push the little people to sit still in crappy restaurants. For the most part, we just didn't do things that were hard.

Some of it was legitimate, of course. When your kids physically outweigh you, there are only so many things you can do, or make them do, and you have to rely primarily on persuasion or terror.

Terror only works if you have the willingness to use it and the awareness of exactly the correct terror to deploy. It may only be a one-shot deal if you aren't willing to follow through. They know you're not going to wallop them once you haven't done it. Forever afterward, the empty threat is just sitting there for comedy. It bears repeating that I totally discourage physical punishment, like walloping, cuffing and excess tickling. These are the last resort of the unimaginative parent. Don't be that parent.

Some people like to compare training children to training dogs. That is beyond ridiculous. Dogs have much better memories.

As your kids march toward adulthood, you must recognize that you will no longer control them, if you ever did. Sure, you can try to manipulate their emotions if you really can't stand all that sudden adulthood. You might offer to feed them when they visit, to soften the whole evolution of admitting they have their own kitchen.

If you try to control their new lives apart from you, it's going to add pressure nobody needs. They do not need your decorating tips for their dorm or their boat. Their space is possibly the first chance they have had to freely express themselves and you don't have to like any of it. If they are decking out their deck to impress you, it's not a great sign of independence.

It's much nicer and more peaceful to just enjoy their company as budding adults and coast into getting yourself fired from control duty.

It's uncomfortable to think about it, but as a parent, you are like that manager who is brought in to fire everyone and shut down the operation. Bit by bit you make yourself obsolete, decommission the play equipment, dispatch the outgrown toys. Don't dwell on it, but remember it when you are inclined to kvetch about your life with kids. In a couple of years, it will all be different and you'll pine for a lot of it.

Self-discipline

Anyway, control yourself!

Without an example, it's entirely possible for a person to grow up without any concept of self-control. That's scarier than an unmaintained ride at the state fair on a windy night. Anything could happen.

You can be a tiny role model for self-discipline, even if your dedication is strictly limited to getting to work on time. It's not enough, but it's a start until you get your own developing brain under better control for larger tricks.

Your kids will notice when you honestly show them your own control struggles. They will take note when you say you'd like to skip folding all the laundry, but you are doing it because leaving it for later will feel worse, and ultimately you would rather not suffocate under a giant laundry monster. They will also notice if you keep bowing out of work because you are too tired or too stressed or too much of a princess.

When it comes to tackling tasks, most of us want it done, but actually we don't want to do the work. So sad! So true! This is why restaurants will always exist. Hooray for food you didn't have to cook!

There's nothing worse than undisciplined discipline. Actually, that's not true—plenty of things are worse, but undisciplined discipline is one of the most destructive forces in a family. It's right up there with its pal, substance abuse.

You can peacefully escort a bull through a china shop; if the bull is sober and well disciplined, the fact that it's a bull becomes basically irrelevant.

If you don't have a grip on your own impulses, it's going to be extremely difficult to help your kids get a grip on their own. If you don't get enough rest because you cannot stop reading some insane pulpy novel, how will you have the energy to make sure that they all get to sleep on time the next night? The little things build up to form bigger things, like leaves in the gutters that will one day flood the front room.

We all have times when it's hard to push ourselves out of a lazy fog to do what needs to be done. How much do you really want to take out the trash instead of pretending it isn't there? It's so negative and oh so normal.

You can acknowledge that you're having a hard time without complaining, at least I have heard rumors about such things. Colorful complaining is a hobby you can indulge in, but don't be surprised when your kids roll around and squeal about every little thing with tremendous drama. They picked that up somewhere.

Purposefully show the kids what's important to you, because you will be showing them anyway by accident. Show them that you care about your time and they will care about their time too, although it may be half past never before they can care about *your* time. (Remember you are Zeus, you are eternal until you are not, etc.)

Among my many faults in time management, I am a world-class snoozer. At times I have had an alarm clock across the room and still managed to snooze it and jump back in bed for an extra half hour of snorts. As a result, half my kids are snoozers too, and the others have found their own ways to give up the pull of extraordinary bed enthusiasm.

One little gal was threatened with an air horn by her stepdad during middle school and still clung fiercely to the fantasy of five more minutes. How she finally beat the snoozing is a mystery to me. I was no help in this.

The fear of being late has not motivated me, in fact I will set my first alarm an hour early just so that I can toy with snoozing. I may tell myself I am happy to have another day and jump out of bed, but on a cold, cloudy morning I will still tap that little line of Zs and celebrate my eyelids for a few rounds. Everyone should be good at something.

Even if, like me, you are a poor example of time control, at least you are an example of what not to do.

Every time you land in the gutter, covered in cookies, you are a cautionary character in somebody's story.

Desserts

The simplest and hardest thing to keep in mind about children and their bad behavior, is remembering to reward the behavior you want to see and never reward the behavior you want to discourage. Ignoring the "bad" behavior is the very best strategy at the start.

Ignoring can be impossible in a crowd of kids, because someone is guaranteed to laugh when the baby discovers arm farts. Arm farts are not inherently bad, of course, but we should point out that they are not in the set of universally accepted behavior, just so everyone understands.

A child who dishes a pile of rice into their pants should be calmly directed to clean up without the reward of entertaining hysteria. Pre-emptively smacking the spoon from their hand doesn't save on the mess and provides them with attention. Make no mistake, they always want attention more than they want sticky pants.

Shielding them from the consequences of their actions should not be a reflex. If they steal from a store, they should personally return the item and apologize as soon as possible. If you are late for work, and the kid has already eaten the hypothetical yogurt, take them back later with the empty carton and an apology. You might want to insist on a toy sacrifice as well, if it's a kid who is immune to embarrassment.

If they get detained for shoplifting, do not immediately rescue them, take your time and have them make their case. If they get suspended from school, do not leave them home with a stack of games and free time galore. If they get caught selling ADHD prescriptions at school, make sure they know how disappointed you are in both their bad judgment and sloppy salesmanship.

It's a balancing act, like virtually every single thing about managing children. You don't want them to get hurt, but you need to remember that they will get hurt. That's life in the real world. It's better they get a bit burned while you are nearby with a fire extinguisher, usually.

We saw a significant change in one little gal when she learned about the value of money. She worked furiously to collect any pocket change she saw for several months. It was an obsession of high comedy. Walking into the living room to find all the cushions askew signaled that she was home from school and making the rounds, scoring quarters.

I gently pointed out that scooping all the change off my dresser wasn't exactly a case for "finders keepers," but otherwise I let the frenzy run its course.

On the day of the book sale at school, she hauled out a huge bag of change and announced that she was taking it to school to buy all the books. When I said that it was too heavy, she ignored me and concealed it in her backpack, and somehow, I failed to notice the jingling or the waddling as she made her way to the bus stop.

The school only made a token effort to alert us before she bought all the books she could afford and gave them to her classmates.

She was deflated when she arrived home again. The spree was a lot of fun, but she had nothing to show for all the hard work and felt terribly let down. I pointed out that she'd made a lot of kids happy.

"But all my money! All my money is gone!"

"That's what happens when you spend money. Once you spend it, it's gone."

Some hot, bitter tears were spent on that fact.

"Look, some people never learn this," I said. "This is great for you. You're only eight!"

Even though it was cold comfort in the moment, she really did learn this lesson in a huge way. For a kid who never seemed to be able to moderate, she put all her wacky energy into moderating herself after that. Pretty much.

Other kids stubbornly spent all their allowance for years before noticing that having a little money to spare felt good. It didn't matter how many times I said it, or how many times I refused to give them a few more dollars to burn. Until they built their own stash of cash, the concept meant nothing to them.

You cannot teach kids to care about their money, but you have to try because they are never going to care about wasting your money.

Screamers

I did not have six screamers. I'm sure it happens, and it must be torture for everyone. Some days, six kids breathing is too much noise. You have to budget your tolerance for such things, just like you budget your money for all the shoes you'll have to buy.

Young children will experiment with screaming and some will keep it up just as long as it's working for them in any way.

We all have experienced the satisfaction of a good howl, because it's the best way to notify the universe, "I'm right here, dummy."

You can't change the fact that there is an element of fun, unless you can. Don't cave to the screamer's whims while they are screaming, and you're half way to peace again.

Older children will scream at times too. They may scream-cry or scream insults or just generally create a cloud of howls. Here's my multiple-choice script—you can use it without attribution at any time: "I can see that you're (upset/angry/disappointed/overwhelmed with *schadenfreude*), but your display is upsetting to other people, so you need to go (upstairs/outside/down to the screaming room) until you're done." Despite being angry enough to bully everyone's eardrums, kids usually don't want to be away from the center of action for very long.

If these methods don't improve the situation in a week, seek professional help for everyone. Screaming, while great for the screamer, is a health hazard to the home.

While it's easy to remember that you need to advocate for your child, you also need to advocate for the rest of humanity at times. When a big kid shoves a smaller kid, you have your chance to explain their responsibility as a bigger kid and advocate for the whole world of smaller kids. They don't know they are bullying until they know.

If you just shrug and say, "Well, that's life in the food chain," you are favoring the bullies. They don't need your help. Speak up, for love and safety.

Expectations

Any time you have expectations, you will usually get better results if you clearly communicate them in advance. Keep it very clear and simple. I had a list I recited before we entered the grocery store: "No shouting, no touching, no running, no fires."

Of course, that's ridiculous and far too negative. I probably should have said, "Walk and whisper, look with your eyes, no fires." Whatever. We never did cause a fire. We did, however, have several incidents that caused our little gang to collect everyone's uncomfortable attention, and we caused a few non-emergency intercom announcements.

What parent has not had a public address system request they collect their naked toddler from the balloon section of the party aisle? I had not instructed her to stay with me and keep her clothes on, so it wasn't exactly against my shopping rules, technically. As I recall, the store had no rule about wearing pants, either.

Once the need for the direction came up, I could add it to the list, "No shouting, stay with me, no touching, no nudity, no running, no fires."

Giving kids a reason for the directions can really help selling them on it, but appealing to their pity will always backfire. If you say, "Mama needs quiet because her head hurts," you'll be all the more irritated when they forget and screech. Kids do not care about your headache until the magical day when they do.

If you are unclear in your messages, the kids will decode your signals. Garbanzo was very pleased to announce when she figured out my pattern: when I said, "We'll see," I meant *No* and, "Maybe later," meant *Yes*. I didn't even know for myself that I hedged so precisely. I shudder to think how many things like that she puzzled out and never told me.

Even if you communicate your expectations with perfect clarity, kids are going to test your limits. It doesn't mean they are bad or that you are ineffective, it's just a drive they have to check things out.

Never forget, your warnings carry information also, and you may give them ideas of stupid things to try. When you say, "Don't put the cat in the dryer," and their little eyes light up with fiendish inspiration, there is really only one fiend here and it's your mouth.

If you are continually threatening and warning them, they will tune you out. Not only is that a blow to your effectiveness, it's infuriating when you begin to realize that your kids are humoring you and ignoring you at the same time. When you catch yourself muttering, "It's your funeral," it may be time to call the reinforcements and take a trip to the movies alone.

If you invent dangers, they will figure it out. That's why it's so important to be credible and measured with your warnings.

You're going to slip up, so forgive yourself for the mistakes in advance.

I have actually said, "Don't eat straight out of the bag," while doing just that with a mouthful of cheese puffs. The joke might have been worth it, but some literal little kid might have their faith shaken by such an incident. You can't please everyone!

Listening

By the time kids are teens, you can only hope that you have given them a sturdy foundation for their next set of adventures. You will not be able to monitor your way out of difficulties. In some situations, monitoring just makes you a witness.

They might have trouble picking helpful friends. It will be hard to watch, but if you don't step back and let them choose, they will miss a chance to hone their skills. Once developed, some of them will be able to teach you how to choose friends better, and wouldn't that be nice?

I spoke frankly with the kids about any topic they cared to discuss and listened to their worries with a sympathetic ear, mostly. Reacting with judgment is going to keep them from confiding faster than snooping in their stuff. Perhaps my biggest misstep was when Pinto Bean confided that she wanted to be a lumberjack. She was trying to sidle up to tell me that she was discovering she was a lesbian and I didn't catch on for a couple of years.

Teens are always confused, perhaps they are the most confused when they claim total certainty. Just because you can take their confusion for granted, that doesn't mean you have license to be condescending. You don't have start every discussion with a phrase like, "Here's how you are being a bonehead." Their bone-headedness doesn't require another remark. It's already submitted into evidence, right alongside yours.

If you don't have any idea what's going on, you might be more comfortable, but you also won't be able to help. I caught myself more than once in realizing I didn't know who my kids were running around with, having forgotten to ask. Not only would I have felt like the worst sort of loser mom when I called the search party, I wouldn't have had anything useful to add to the hunt.

Nobody disappeared, much. They didn't tell me everything, but they claim that they never felt like there was anything they could not talk about with me.

I was frank about drugs, maybe a bit too much. It seemed to me that the big mistake parents made in drug education was teaching the ancient method of "Just Say No."

They asked a lot of questions and I affirmed that yes, people do drugs because it's fun. Getting high can feel great! It can feel like a vacation from your own life, and everyone likes a vacation. The problems come when you have to pay for the vacation and come home again a little poorer, a little more sleepless and a lot more apart from your life.

I emphasized that dabbling should be done with a good understanding. Don't just take a thing that someone hands you, assuming your friends know something you don't. Safety first. If a chemical kills brain cells, why would you dabble with that? You need your brains more than they need you.

The other main thing with teens is trying to keep them busy enough that they don't slide into destructive habits, but not so busy that they don't have time to screw up and learn things the hard way. Arts! Sports! Musics! There's a reason they are a big part of secondary school. When there aren't enough activities, kids will always find time to catch chlamydia, or worse.

Teaching

Because they may not get it in school, it's up to you to teach your kids how to think rather than focusing on what to think. Because you are the adult and have huge jumpstart on them, you can always sway them, but it's a risky move. Some kids will sense that you are pressing a particular agenda and they will swing the other way, hard.

If you show them how to think critically about information, they will use this against you in an argument, so it might seem like a self-defeating strategy. What? Are they you? No, they are not you. Knock it off, and teach your kids how to evaluate evidence logically.

Kids who just accept whatever they read can get into very weird trouble faster than ever before. I was one of those kids. I loved to read about fringe supernatural experiences and all sorts of baloney and those authors really had me going. I was ripe for some cult to scoop me up and scoop out my brains.

Consider it cult-proofing when you show them how undue influence works. You will save a ton of money in therapy and kidnapping expenses.

With my kids, I would quiz them regularly on television commercials. Assuming advertisements aren't going away any time soon, they make an excellent sandbox for critical assessment. "What are they selling?" I would ask while the little spuds were watching a ketchup commercial. I did my best to make sure they understood that something was being sold, wrapped up in a shiny package of friendship and fun or—gasp— sexual satisfaction.

That's obvious, right? Sure, but not to kids and not to everyone who was a kid. Most people are still wide-open and accepting of these messages at vulnerable moments, like when they have become run-down or have taken a fast-acting sleeping pill. Anyone who has ever done some late-night drunk shopping knows what I am describing here. We didn't actually need twelve pillows with Nicolas Cage's face on them, now did we?[15]

Kids who ask "why" all the time are a pain in the butt, but they aren't just your pain in the butt. Those kids are getting ready to deal with unreasonable bureaucratic nonsense and pushy persons who will do them dirty. They are going to need all those "whys" in the future.

Kids who listen to song lyrics and ask, "Wait, isn't there some creepy subtext here about predatory obsession?" Well, those kids might get punched in the arm during band practice, but they will also be immunized from weird cultural cues. Better that than having a child who chants lyrics that they don't

---

[15] Nicolas Cage is a versatile yet debated film actor whose likeness really fills a pillowcase.

understand who then gets punched in the face for something else they don't understand.

If you begin to wonder what your kids truly understand about anything, there is a simple method for investigating: ask them to explain it to you and just listen. Don't make faces or noises, just let the information roll all over the place and see what they unfurl for you. Some of the greatest conversations of my whole silly life started with asking my kids to teach me. I may never need to know what happens when a dungeon design is too complex, but if I ask about it with an open mind, I'll know that they know.

This is every bit as helpful with small kids, too. Ask them to teach you how and you'll find out what they actually learned.

Surprises

Whatever method of modelling discipline you choose, your kids will surprise you. If you are super casual, you will probably have at least one kid who demands structure and pushes you to promise things whether you are sure you can deliver or not. Don't fall for it.

Even if, by some miracle, you show them excellent self-control, you are not their only source. They are going to try out other ideas too. They may begin to decide that they know better than you do, based on absolutely nothing at all.

When your middle schooler says, "There, there, Mother," you can be pretty sure she's getting her ethos from Looney Tunes[16], so pay attention. Nobody wants that. Shouts of, "suffering succotash!" would clinch the case. In this situation, hide your anvils, naturally.

It is delicate to balance and determine how much control will backfire. Typically, if you exert too much control, they are going to react in a way that demands more and more control until nobody can enjoy anything.

If you aren't controlling, odds are some of your kids will start trying to control you. You can have fun teaching them how much they cannot control you, but maybe don't have too much fun with that at their expense.

You still want them to stop by for brunch a couple of decades later on, don't you?

Garbanzo was always an inventor. She would put ice cubes in her own shirt, to practice hiding her reactions. At the time, I had no idea all those puddles in the kitchen were so productive. She may have hidden the exercise she invented from me, thinking I would object, but had I known, I would have made extra ice.

It's not that we should encourage them to hide all their feelings—that fashion has passed. Developing the ability to choose when and how to react to ice cubes and other insults will always make them more employable.

---

[16] Looney Tunes was revived from a long-running cartoon series that entertained children with violent imagery and stereotypes of barnyard animals, so essentially the preliminary to the internet.

Chapter 13
The Mistake of Caring About Housework

Growing up, I have discovered over time, is rather like housework: never finished.
–Lois McMaster Bujold

Everyone has different levels of dedication to tidiness and dustiness. I am a fairly dusty type and have been distressed by my nature for my whole life. Until now.

Acceptance

I have a robot vacuum, and we clean together while everyone makes fun of us. My robot vacuum understands. It sometimes dances and spins in circles for a few long minutes and then gives up, chiming and screeching, "Error!"

I get it. This is exactly my pattern for housecleaning, too.

When I first piled in with the kids' stepdad, I enjoyed the calm and cleanliness of his home. If people showed up, there was no hot burst of shame at the state of the living room. It was fine, all the time. What a nice way to live. It is not, however, my natural way. I am a dust pig.

Being a dust pig can be acceptable, if you can accept it.

I fought that acceptance for many years, and noticing my own short-comings became a very burdensome hobby.

Visiting professionally maintained spaces, I see all the rough edges now. Corners, baseboards, streaky windows, I notice it all like a hospitality inspector. What a misery. I miss the days when I was oblivious to cobwebs and clutter.

Even as a dust pig, I have some standards. I will not tolerate mice or bugs or old food. Piles of discarded shoes distress me, piles of books do not. Toys sprinkled around the room feel festive, but pens and markers worry me. They could spring a leak and spray ruin on innocent objects. Things that could choke a pet or person get picked up even if I'm in a hurry, so knight me!

If you can have a robot vacuum or a nice person come and help you clean up from time to time, count yourself lucky. If you can find some joy in sorting through junk and making space to live with extra joy on top, good for you.

By all means, teach your kids how to care for their things and spaces. I never learned the skills in my youth, so we figured many things out together.

Our work parties were notoriously tough. Tears and tantrums were routine. If I ever wanted to clear a room of people, I could casually mention basement clean-up and sit back and watch the evacuation.

Are they better off for having been nagged relentlessly about putting things away and washing up? I should probably ask them, but I'm reluctant to start anything.

With so many kids, it was necessary to badger them to hang up their stuff. Otherwise the mountain of backpacks and shoes at the end of a school day looked like both an emergency and a fire hazard.

Part of the reason I was raised a dust pig was because I was the only kid around. It wasn't hard to pick up my discarded socks; there were usually only two at a time. I believe any only child is the most likely to become a messy adult for this reason.

My mother said that she didn't want to make me clean toilets because she knew that once I started, I would never stop. That's not to say that I would be a perpetual scrubber, but that the housework is endless.

It is true, if you have a house, you are going to have housework. Even if you avoid the work of housework, eventually you have to clear a path or mop up some mysterious stickiness because you cannot stand the mystery any longer.

Don't worry yourself needlessly. There isn't very much required to keep the authorities from interfering in your way of slovenly life. I wouldn't know exactly where the limit is, mind you, but if you take out the trash, keep your roof and drainage in good order, and keep your yard from harboring vermin, you are somewhere above that lower limit.

Is that what you want to pass along to your kids? Maybe demonstrate a few helpful techniques now and then. You can remind them that it's usually easier to prevent a mess than to clean it up, just like someone who cares about a clean house would.

By no means am I suggesting that you bully your kids into an immaculate way of life. Of course, I didn't do that, but I've witnessed that approach and the after effects. Kids who are terrorized with cleanliness can become phobic about germs and obsessive about cleanliness. Just calm down, everyone. Dirt happens, and clean up can be predictable and boring, instead of a grand, tragic opera.

If you have chronically reluctant little cleaners, it is one of the few situations where I recommend saddling up the shame horse. Once your kids are old enough to become self-conscious, you can ask them how they would feel if their hero saw their bedroom. For some kids the mere idea of Spider Man coming to town is enough to motivate them, while others will only get moving with the imminent threat of a visit by Amy from next door.

You can decide for yourself how worthwhile threats of Spider Amy may be.

Putting housekeeping at the very lowest priority for my entire parenting career made having many dogs and cats possible. It was fine. Sure, we were embarrassed when a tumbleweed of fur blew into the foyer as company arrived. And yes, I clutched my imaginary pearls on occasion, when a new victim asked to use our bathroom for the first time. Would there be tissue? Was the sink full of paint brushes and naked dolls? Doll heads only?

My absolute base line turned out to be safety. When my kids spent half a winter playing the Nose Mirror Game, I only wanted the house to be trip resistant.

As far as I know, the Nose Mirror Game was their own invention. To play, you walk around the house looking down at a plastic hand mirror under your nose. This provides a near hallucination that you are walking on the ceiling and you may feel you are going to trip over things that aren't in your actual physical dimension.

To play safely, the obstacles in your path have to be predictable. A discarded towel at the top of the stairs could cause a horrible wipe out. They understood that clearing the decks was a pre-condition of the game and eventually the cat did, too.

Professionals

Using professional tools and hiring professional help whenever possible might spare your family some avoidable pain. I wept through many window washing episodes before I discovered squeegees.

If you really have no clue how to attack cleaning, watch some professionals. They do not putter and they do not dab. They get in there get it done and get out again.

If you hate to dust, then you have the option to keep people out of your house or keep less stuff in your house that collects dust. You want a chandelier? Cool. Can you clean it without creating a chemical haze? There's so much to consider if you care about being clean.

If you hire people to clean, bear in mind that your children will not learn anything except how to watch other people deal with their messes. It's not a great experience, as experiences go. My kids got to overhear a cleaner bitterly complain about how dirty they were and they did not take it to heart, but instead concluded that she was mean. The dog really disliked her, so that was probably valid.

Another cleaner would habitually put the parmesan cheese can with the janitorial supplies. I never saw her scour the sink with parmesan, but that might be what kept the confusion going. Library books got shelved, too. Fines occurred.

All things considered, I'd say clean with the kids and spend the cleaner wages on pizza and nonsense rewards.

Tools

It's important to have a method to insure that you never have to call an inquisition to find a scrub brush, pair of working tweezers, a hammer, scissors, a flashlight or anything else that would cause you to get mad enough to interrogate all the children within earshot.

Even when the children are wise to the technique it still works, since it is founded on their natural laziness and optimism.

Hide your tools and use decoys.

Any child will take the first pair of scissors found, even if it's not the sharpest pair, because they instantly convince themselves that they can make it work well enough. Optimism.

They know there are better tools, probably in the very back of the same drawer, but they will not go to the extra trouble to dig them out. Laziness.

It is groovy when psychology is our friend.

It's tempting to fingerprint the tools that spontaneously re-appear, but why bother? You got your tweezers back and you don't really want to know the origin of the gunk on the screwdriver, do you?

Enjoy your own cleverness, but don't be too smug. Regardless of how proficient you are at squirreling your tools, once in a while, a kid will barge into your cocktail party waiving your vibrator around and complaining that it is the worst flashlight ever.

It is to be expected.

Checklist

We had checklists posted in most of the rooms of the house. One way to be sure that kids will never read a checklist is to have a checklist. "How to clean the bathroom in 15 minutes" is my favorite one that they ignored. The fifteen-minute routine was done on occasion, and it usually took more time than that.

Framing the chores as a tiny slice of time is a great trick to play on yourself and children who haven't caught on yet. Tell them to give the job five minutes. Just get started and you're suddenly 51% done.

Most checklists would be even more effective if step one was "take Adderall." Unfortunately, stimulants have a tendency to bork up your whole day afterward.

I found checklists effective when I began to feel that no one else was matching my paltry level of effort. I drew them up and they were enthusiastically adopted for a few days before we reached the stage in which everyone pretended never to have heard of the checklist.

A few of the kids have gone on to develop their own checklists. They are the ones I would allow to drive my space shuttle.

Behold! A basic cleaning checklist:

- Step one: Be hydrated and or medicated.
- Step two: Locate your tools and equipment. The last thing you want is for your little helper to wander off and look for window spray in a tree.
- Step three: Remember to start from somewhere, usually from the top. It doesn't matter if you go clockwise or not, just choose. Maybe you're left-handed and are convinced you should proceed counter-clockwise. If so, congratulations on having nailed a decision in advance!
- Step four: Decide what being done looks like. If you really only have that fifteen minutes, maybe being done means there are no obvious fur balls or dust.

You are in charge of your space and you are in charge of exactly how much you care about housework. Be nice to yourself in any case. Those dishes will not do themselves, truly, but you don't have to suffer over the sink twice.

Fun

There are people who find a way to make housework fun and others who manage to make it gratifying, at least that is a persistent rumor I have heard. You can make it fun for little kids, if you remove the pressures of time and results.

Eventually, even a three-year-old will groan when you sing a clean-up song one time too many. It's hard to keep having new ideas when there are so many days and so many chores to conquer.

Because we are not usually Mary Poppins, each of us needs to hunt down our neighborhood Mary Poppins for tips. She's out there. She's making her own tortillas and ironing pleats in things and doing it all without grimness and recrimination. I believe in her, and while I'm pretty sure I cannot be like her, I can get some ideas.

She may have a knack for getting kids to want to help her sort socks or peel potatoes. She might flatter them on even the most bogus efforts to win them over. She is full of tricks.

The thing is, when you find her, you'll learn she doesn't have to report to anyone, she's setting her own schedule and her own priorities and that's why she's not pissed off all the time. If her home is presentable and hospitable, I guarantee there are toys crammed under her couch. Don't point it out. She'll pretend to mind, even though she obviously does not.

You can teach the kids to clean up or you can wait until they are asleep and squander your quiet time on pushing that laundry mountain up the hill one more time.

You can Poppins with the time you have, or not, there's no wrong answer. You don't have to care what anybody else thinks. How do you want to live? Are you content with your home as it is? Could you be?

Chapter 14
The Mistake of Modeling Addiction

When the going gets weird, the weird turn pro
– Hunter S. Thompson

I had a memorable conversation with one of my gals about setting examples. She asked me why a dad would behave so badly in front of his kids. The dad in question had a very colorful meltdown complete with throwing objects and frenzied exaggerations delivered at maximum volume.

Demonstrations

My gal was indignant about it, in a very 13-year-old manner. "He's setting such a bad example." She fidgeted as she spoke.

"Sometimes," I said, "the example people provide is what not to do."

She was satisfied with this answer beyond my grandest hopes.

With this idea of the anti-model firmly in mind, I decided to start drinking in earnest, to show them how it is not to be done. My previous time on the wagon wasn't inoculating them the way my own parents' behavior had inoculated me, I thought.

I don't actually remember my dad as a drunk, but he only had weekends to work with. My mother, on the other hand, had some horrible episodes. I recall thinking that she had parked her brain somewhere else and let some other entity take the wheel. At her worst, she might have slapped me for laughing at music. To this day, I still refuse to laugh at music, so I guess it wasn't a wasted trauma—assuming it happened, of course.

Both my parents had quit drinking and joined sobriety communities by the time I was a teenager.

Their sobriety had not caused mine, in fact, I spent a lot of my high school years intoxicated. Once it was legal for me to drink, however, the allure vanished and I stopped seeing any point to liquor.

Not only did I have ambivalence about alcohol, I was a bit of a foe of booze. In an earlier era, I might have been cheering on a Carrie Nation[17] character as she smashed up bars with her hatchet.

I was in a bind once my own teenagers had started to have run-ins with drinking. Mung Bean had

––––––––––––––––––

[17] Carrie Nation very famously ran around smashing up saloons with a hatchet. This was before liquor was briefly and unsuccessfully prohibited in the U.S. during a time when people smashed things with hatchets without much penalty.

shockingly guzzled two bottles of wine and confessed all her secrets from the bathroom floor. She had also destroyed the living room carpet with the resulting sickness. We were all very impressed by the idiocy.

I had always believed that children wouldn't eat or drink themselves sick, and while that is true for most children, there's always one like her who has to learn the hard way by waking up in the hospital after a binge of pastries and champagne.

They need to witness some poor decisions, I thought, in order to avoid personally visiting every pitfall. I could model some drinking, I thought. So, I did.

If I have been guilty of a more magnificent rationalization, I don't know what it is, but it probably caused a person.

Over the course of a decade, I traveled from a dislike of losing control of my faculties to a flirtation with brain damage. Irish livers are a miraculous thing. The false courage they provide is a source of misery for generations.

It's possible my kids benefited and were a bit less likely to over-indulge, but I could have made them sit through a few films to accomplish the same effect, while keeping all my brain cells, I bet.

Addiction

Any addiction can teach kids about how addiction works. It doesn't matter if it's games or chemicals, if it's a habit that serves as a hideout, it deserves self-regulation.

Lima Bean had a compulsion to collect every flavor of a weird lip balm that was shaped like an egg. Telling her that they were not actually flavors, but different color packaging didn't help. Reasoning couldn't touch her impulse. The other kids were eager to help her do it, too. As soon as the collection was complete, the next pointless project could take hold.

Pokemon were the same deal. Do you really *gotta catch 'em all?* How much time is that going to take? Do you really have the time to spare for all that catching?

A diversion is only harmless when there is zero harm. Wasting your time and energy is not zero harm.

Technology

We explained to a young one that her cell phone was not a baby and watched her mourn when her imaginary pets died imaginary deaths. She learned nothing from the episode.

Later the kids were all upset when her imaginary character drowned and they had to watch its imaginary dad mourn by the pool every time they played the game. Did they quit the game? Of course not. They drowned even more characters with the special sort of covert glee that only nice kids have.

It's no wonder that some parents are strongly against technology, but it doesn't really change the basic problem that kids are not great at regulating their own behavior, until they are.

I remember spending summer days trying to keep a badminton birdie up in the air for a record-setting number of bounces. Sure, that's 19th century technology, so it seems cuter, but it's not really much different than trying to get a high score on an electronic game.

If your kid is tense and working through some difficult phase, which is most of them most of the time, they could probably use a little hide-out. If it becomes an obsession, you will all know.

There was a phase during which Garbanzo would race home to watch "The Three Stooges" after school. She had never even acknowledged black and white television before and the intensity worried me. By the time I figured out that she was just trying to solve comedy and violence at the same time, the phase was over—and if it was an obsession, it was too quick to count.

Soy Bean went bananas for baseball statistics but never had any interest in actually playing the game. The numbers and the notebooks filled with numbers were the point for her.

I tried to remember the abstract nature of obsessing when Pinto Bean was learning all about European history from a video game assassin's viewpoint. Fortunately, none of the kids have shown any interest in actually shooting anything or hurling themselves off rooftops into tiny bales of hay.

Most of these things just need time to resolve themselves. That gives you time to focus on the obsessions that stick around.

The phone compulsion is a bit more universal, and it can be dangerous. If I had ever imagined that my own mother would have the ability to send me random thoughts at all hours, I think I would have put more effort into convincing her that smart phones were radioactive.

Having a device which *dings* and causes a pleasant startle every time, even though it is not bringing you a delicious snack, well, that is just not okay and we all understand that.

A notification could be a vote of confidence or a death threat. Why does it feel good? It feels good because sometimes it is good news. It's not always your neighbor telling you she has a fungus. Sometimes it's a robot showing approval for a message you sent out last year, or an actual friend telling you they like the haircut you don't have any longer. It is something encouraging just often enough to keep you feeling encouraged by the *ding*.

Developments

Really, working on your addictions will save you a lot of time and if you are actively saving your time, at least you aren't wasting it on absolutely nothing.

If you are drugging yourself up every spare moment, you are missing out on some prime free time, as well as the time you need to look around and realize your home is actually a dumpster.

Your addictions may provide solace from some painful emotions. Everyone understands that, I bet.

You know you've overdone it when you forget what pain feels like. It's like being so well-fed that you don't recall, really recall in detail, what hunger feels like.

You have to feel some pain now and then. It is literally the way that life works. You are born, you feel pain, you learn things, you stay born until you are not. Then it's over and you wonder where all the time went.

Do you want to be pretty confident that it all went up in smoke?

If you keep hiding in the substances, you'll never have the gumption to master your dysfunction. You may find yourself arguing with people about how you simply cannot accept the concept of a Higher Power. You will not realize when you do so that you are letting them know you kind of believe you may not have a higher power because you are it. Very embarrassing.

Your kids take note of all the things you say and do, particularly your habits that don't make any sense. They see the way you count out spare change to pay for that pack of cigarettes and the way you disdain a relative who gambles as you buy a fistful of lottery tickets.

If you are sneaking around to do these things, they still know about it. When daddy has a computer full of porn, the only people who don't know it are the ones who don't believe porn is real.

You are not fooling anyone with your perfume bottle full of gin, either.

We all want to believe that in the correct formulation of circumstances we could, quite readily, transform into a super spy. We could beat the lie detector or slip into a side office undetected if the stakes were high enough.

Embarrassment does not make high stakes for everyone. We're just trying to get away with a little something we think the universe should allow us to have, like stealing a bite of food from a full buffet.

But what if the buffet is really unhealthy and full of things like cancer and poverty and shame? Do we still want to steal from it? Of course. We are all on team pervert, after all. We want free stuff, even if it's really awful free stuff.

I watched people I dearly love stagger and fall under the influence of their particular poison. They stared back unsteadily while I recited to them a list of their mistakes. I have interrupted them in the thrall of a chemically induced fit of mania, when they decided to take up a new craft, which they had just invented, which required sharp tools and skill they didn't have, even when they were momentarily sober.

Drunkards generally believe they are artists, and they are adept at convincing themselves they are deeply talented, just like people under the influence get a burst of confidence that makes them believe they are performing better while high. This isn't true for driving, in fact, it is only true for comedy, and even then, it only works for some of the comedians some of the time.

So, I have counseled many clowns, and finally when I had plenty of time and practice, I found that I was one of those clowns myself.

Women can't drink as much as men, it turns out. Our livers are smaller and simply will not put up with the same level of bullshit.

One friend who was decades sober told me that in her work she had seen it over and over again: women crash hard and fast. They do not get the same number of chances that men do. Their organs have a meeting and will *adios* before their brain makes it to the party, and that's a really sad party.

For some reason, there is little official consensus on how much one can drink before their drinking is unsafe, and that is because zilch is the only safe dose. A lady may wrinkle her nose at a glass of zilch, because it doesn't have that bouquet of tasty danger.

She may go on to pour herself a serving or three of the anti-zilch in the evening because the wild side is her area. That's fine. I did that, too. But I had a deal with myself. I didn't kid myself about the way I was toasting to my own brain damage and I weighed my wine to keep myself honest with myself about how much I was not zilching. Attempting to lie to yourself out in the open is appalling and hilarious.

I did not accept that I was powerless over alcohol. Alcohol and I were shaking hands until my hands started shaking themselves.

Rationalizations make the worst poetry, I bet.

Freedom

The kids will notice when you begin to get a grip on your diversions, but don't expect applause.

When I quit smoking for good, I remember being peeved when all the people who had harped at me to quit were not continuously praising me. It was my struggle and while they were presumably happy for me, they weren't in the congratulating business. Bummer.

The best addiction quitting advice I ever heard: the urge will pass regardless of what you do. This is true for every type of urge.

Many people substitute a new habit for the old one. They quit smoking tobacco, but incessantly pick up cigarette-shaped objects and chew on them. They may begin to eat too much when they no longer drink too much alcohol. Maybe they give up sex for Bingo and then move on from Bingo to scarier thrill seeking. It's natural, but it's a good idea to be aware of what you are doing.

You may end up demonstrating all this for your kids, and they need to see what doesn't work just as well as what does work. Share the positive milestones because you totally shared your low points, even if you don't remember them.

You can show them how you free yourself of bad habits, unhealthy occupations, toxic friendships and dim ideas. Talk is fine, but showing them how you travel from imaginable to tangible improvements in your life will school them in hope better than a bra full of chickens.

Chapter 15
Conclusion

Peace is this moment without judgment
– Dorothy Hunt

For many of us, we reach a point where we realize we have made some mistakes. It's painful. What if we had accepted that scholarship? What if we had rejected that scholar?

Admissions

The point to keep firmly in mind is that you did what you did because you did what you did. Move along. You can apologize to yourself and others and try to make better decisions in the future. It's tempting to swirl in a state of wondering about the alternatives that didn't happen, but I recommend only short vacations in the Land of What Ifs.

If I had not made mistakes, I would have had fewer kids, probably. I wouldn't change the outcome now—it's a terrible and impossible thing to regret a whole person or a whole bunch of persons.

We aren't responsible for everything that goes wrong, but we are responsible when we go wrong. On top of that we are the only humans who can give ourselves a break about the breakage. Only we can forgive the things only we know. Our hearts are for us to heal. It's a huge bonus if we can let God and other experts help.

For me, I had to truly forgive myself before I could begin to forgive anyone else for past shenanigans. It is not tidy and the forgiveness is not complete. Forgiveness is more of an ongoing project, like mowing the lawn.

As time passes, you have fewer opportunities to make things right or to improve your relationships with your kids. You can stall in blame and at all sorts of other stations on the relationship railroad, but I recommend working on it now. Clearing up your communications and keeping things real for everyone makes space for a loving future.

Alienation

If they aren't speaking to you, ask them why and believe what they tell you, even if it's very bad news for your ego or your therapy budget.

Admitting that you have made mistakes with your kids is painful, maybe excruciating. Understanding your mistakes is not going to be painful forever if you face it and sit with it and accept it, the way you would accept a three-legged dog at a bus stop.

You weren't perfect and that's okay.

Really.

They are allowed to be mad at you for whatever it was.

What you do now matters a whole lot more, now that you know better.

Once they are grown, your only unfinished business is the business of kindness. Not the reflexive polite sort of kindness, but the genuine, steady sort of kindness. If you haven't mastered it yet, it's not too late to learn. Old dogs learn plenty of tricks, including how to make humans carry them around.

You will never fix your relationship with your kids by trying to fix them. Simply making the attempt to fix another person is inviting judgment into the middle of the conversation. Judgment is only getting in your way and judgment is never going to keep you warm at night. I tried it and it's not at all cozy.

The thing that seems like an error on their part may not be wrong for them. It may seem like a mistake to you because it doesn't align with your expectations of what they should want or should do. A disappointment for you is not necessarily a mistake for them. Perhaps you could simmer down with all that fix-it energy.

Have you ever attempted to fix someone's poor taste in films or music? It's exactly like that. You can't even try to improve their taste without a starting point of assuming you know what's better for them.

Guess what? You don't know what's best for them. You may have hunches, but they belong to you.

One magical day, they may ask for your opinion and then you can unfurl all those wacky theories and see what sort of reception they get. If you trot them out prematurely, a poor reception is all but guaranteed.

As adults, they don't need your approval, but your acceptance is a crucial way to love them as adults and it's worth all the work it may require.

If you can accept yourself, you can accept them and it's likely going to be a great big acceptance party, which you started by inviting yourself.

Pointers

As a blueprint for the benefit of people who prefer lists, here are my main pointers in parenting. They have varying levels of difficulty and possibility.

- Only marry someone who will make an awesome ex-partner
- Grow up before you have kids and make your mental and emotional health top priority
- Be financially independent first and stay there
- Only have kids if you are very serious about having kids for life
- Learn from others as much as you learn from yourself
- Help kids recognize their emotions and accept their own feelings with kindness
- Be truthful, especially when it's personally embarrassing
- Be kind (that should probably be pointer number one)
- Show kids how to be a helpful human
- Teach kids how to think, not what to think
- Listen to kids, especially when you don't want to listen
- Interfere as little as you can and let kids make choices
- Explore together as much as possible
- Find the fun

For some reason, humans have a tendency to complicate things and forget other things. It is possible to forget to be kind, or to lose your way and misplace your sense of respect for yourself and others.

It's up to you to find a way to remember who you are and what your mission is. Perhaps take some time every morning to align yourself with your future self. Maybe don't dive into doing any chores until you remember why you are doing them today.

While you are younger, you have the best opportunity to get a grip on yourself, because you may never again have this much energy. Your emotions can carry you along or carry you away.

Fortunately, if you don't get a handle on your emotional rudder at first, you can always do it later and the current isn't as strong. As you age, it is trickier, however. There can be emotional mythical beasts under the surface.

Self-help can be insufficient once there are sea monsters and such. If you suspect your support system might not be up to the safest sea monster wrangling operation, call in some professionals. You deserve enough help and you can always ask for help finding help. Everyone needs therapy at some point. Just because they don't consider it, that doesn't mean it's not needed.

Big Tree Parenting

I haven't come up with a better name for it. *Passive Parenting* and *Peaceful Parenting* are taken and they don't represent the collection of parenting ideas I favor here on the other side, anyway. Slow Parenting may be the closest thing.

If we approach parenting like a big tree, that means first of all we are mature on our own, steady and patient, and quite limited in the actions we can do to influence our surroundings. We have powerful effects, just by being there. We offer shade and shelter, food and comfort and above all we listen.

A Big Tree does not jeer or judge or pour out its insecurities to those under its shade. It doesn't hide its flaws or its struggles. It does not pretend to be something else. It also does not move every three years.

I know people aren't trees as well as you do and I know this doesn't cover everything, but I will stand right here and tell you with all my big tree earnestness that it is a great image to call on in moments of doubt and difficulty. When a toddler is pulling on you for the fortieth time in forty seconds and you feel the steam building in your ears, just ask yourself if you can be the Big Tree for one more second. When your teen bounds into your room with news right after you started to drift off to sleep and you are righteously flooded with irritation and can't decide if you should yell or listen, consider your Big Tree life.

Through all the accidental and incidental events of raising my kids, I believe that my inertia and even my laziness was a tremendous gift to them. By failing to be a dynamo of control, I happened to give them space and time to become the people they are. Some people would say they became the people they already were, and I agree with those people at least halfway.

Parents can hang back and use their energy to be a coach rather than a boss. Gentle nudges can accomplish a full change of course over time, and we don't have to hurry if we stay in touch with our little floaty boats.

Being a Big Tree Parent isn't easy much of the time, so even if it seems lazy or potentially pandering, it's also a real job of work. Think of the security guard who languishes in the empty bank lobby. She has nothing to do until she does. It's hard to just be there and not wander off or drum up drama or rob things.

Having a parent who is present is more than many people ever have. If you aren't physically present you can't possibly be emotionally and mentally present with your kids. If you can be physically, emotionally and mentally present most of the time you have an excellent start on the hardest and most worthy work of your whole Big Tree life.

Trust

Throughout my entire early parenting career, I was continuously rolling with the internal monologue, "I can't handle this," while I was, in fact, handling it.

One minor nervous breakdown and I decided I wasn't really as strong as I had always believed. I was mistaken: I was that strong, maybe stronger. It took a lot of time and reflection to understand.

Understanding could only happen much later when I was responsible for a sane number of people. Being responsible for a greater number of people than you have hands is a recipe for juggling. Juggling for decades takes an awful lot of energy and boy oh boy can you drop some things.

I wonder now how much better our lives would have been if I had been telling myself, "I've got this," in more situations, if I had not been afraid to trust myself in so many others.

Your ability to love yourself and your kids will grow with practice.

If you don't believe in your ability to love your family, who will?

There were intervals when family life felt like a hostage situation, and I know I'm not alone in that experience. The really dire and dark times can inspire some terrible ideas, but we can also remember that we have the ransom, we always have more choices than the first thing we notice. We can take a minute or five to breathe and consider other options.

Asking for help may seem like an unwanted complication when we're in the worst places, but try to remember that people love to help, even the people who love to help primarily so that they can feel they are superior, heroic characters in their own story. Whatever. They will still help you get your baby to the hospital.

I remember watching another mom of too many who had a wonderful, centered ambiance about her, and I wanted nothing more than to carry her off for coffee and learn all her secrets. Now I understand that there are no secrets, there are only difficulties we don't want to accept that look a little like secrets. Being dedicated to love, bravery and sanity might have been what that mom was doing. If it was something else, I need to read her book.

We all want to get this right and provide a better life for our kids than we had—at least I would argue that all good parents want that—and most bad parents want that too. Some folks simply lack the tools to build that better life. Others are blindsided by hardships and can't get back on the life raft or even begin to steer it.

The best parents are always second-guessing themselves and making decisions while holding their noses in uncertainty. Trust that if you are trying your best, you are definitely not the worst.

Think about all the times you have fretted and everything was okay in the end. You can tell yourself, "It will be okay," and you will almost always be right.

Then you get to be right and okay. How marvelous!!

Regrets

Apologies are overrated. They are hard to do well, and they don't always smoothly progress to a nice tidy improvement of whatever it is. It's possible to study your audience and craft an excellent apology that still leaves everyone mildly uncomfortable and ill-equipped to order lunch with their usual self-assurance.

Maybe that's just me again.

"Forgive me," is a pretty shitty apology. It's more of an order, or if delivered with great tenderness, a strong suggestion that doesn't outline the specifics at all. You're going to need more words to tell the truth, keep it clear, and apologize like a pro.

Do not excavate ancient civilizations in your set up. If your apology begins with, "Throughout history," just stop. You've detoured into word salad territory and need to get a lot more relevant.

Recently, I gave a very successful apology and I may stick with that method for the rest of my life. I said, "I thought I had really good reasons, but it was a terrible idea, and I was entirely wrong." I'm sure an expert linguist would point out that there's no "sorry" in there, but the sorry in the tone was plenty. I'm pretty sure. Nobody likes to be wrong and 110% of people dislike being entirely wrong.

Now, when I have those bubbles of regret, I have lunch with a kid and apologize for my shortcomings. I always let them order food before I get rolling (see above, if you already forgot why).

The kids find the apologies alarming at first because they imagine I am going to say something much stranger than, "I'm sorry I didn't listen to you enough when you were in middle school."

Their flashes of distress can be entertaining.

So far, the kids brush off my apologies. Often, they say they prefer their version of events as if we remember different histories.

Regrets are often like some funny looking imaginary friend that no one else recalls at all. As a side effect of raising a pack of kind kids, the kids' memories are so very, very kind.

It's worth the effort to try to offer the apologies, aside from the aforementioned entertainment, particularly if you want to continue to stay connected. There is always a chance that some kid didn't know that going to seven different schools is not ideal, or they may not know that you regret setting that in motion.

They may not remember the way you were marooned that time you started a survival fire and fueled it with breastfeeding pads. Whatever happens, everyone notices different things.

They may blame you for a while, but blame is usually temporary. If they do blame you, at least blame means they have standards.

When you have made as many mistakes as I have, you begin to see you can only cringe for so long before stumbling on some compassion. We do our best, even when we do it badly.

I know now that all the times I fell short, my kids were given the chance to get taller.

Thank you for reading!!

Feel free to follow my blog on askyermom.com or my parenting essays on askyermom.substack.com.

Have questions? Found a typo? Want to embarrass me and my dead proofreader? Just email mom@askyermom.com.

Bask in your pretty good parenting!!

You are doing great work, even if it's only pretty good!!

Love,

yermom